Manifesting Peace

Manifesting Peace

Twelve Principles for Cultivating Peace, Healing,
and Wellness Distilled from the World's
Spiritual Traditions and Psychology

JAMES S. ANDERSON

WIPF & STOCK · Eugene, Oregon

MANIFESTING PEACE
Twelve Principles for Cultivating Peace, Healing and Wellness Distilled
from the World's Spiritual Traditions and Psychology

Wipf & Stock
An Imprint of Wipf and Stock Publishers
199 W. 8th Ave., Suite 3
Eugene, OR 97401

www.wipfandstock.com

PAPERBACK ISBN: 978-1-5326-7055-8
HARDCOVER ISBN: 978-1-5326-7056-5
EBOOK ISBN: 978-1-5326-7057-2

Manufactured in the U.S.A.   JANUARY 22, 2019

This work is dedicated to my nephews whom I love very much and pray the peace of God will always accompany. May this book fall into the hands of those needing more peace, helping reorient them toward God, thus advancing his kingdom.

All that is written in the Torah was written for the sake of peace.

(TANHUMA, SHOFETIM 18)

For God is a God not of disorder, but of peace.

(1 COR 14:33)

Peace I leave with you; my peace I give to you. I do not give to you as the world gives. Do not let your hearts be troubled, and do not let them be afraid.

(JOHN 14:27)

The Lord give you peace.

ST. FRANCIS OF ASSISI'S GREETING TO ALL, EVEN IN THE FACE OF CRUELTY AND VIOLENCE.

But he was pierced for our transgressions, he was crushed for our iniquities; the punishment that brought us peace was on him, and by his wounds we are healed.

(ISA 53:5)

Peace begins with a smile.

MOTHER TERESA

Contents

Preface

PEACE PROVES ILLUSIVE FOR many of us today in our increasingly busy lives and world, but what is articulated here can bring more of it than we currently have if implemented even in part.

Brevity and an economy of words are thus aimed for in what follows: a synthesis of wisdom and insights from the world's religious traditions and spiritual giants within the field of psychology and counseling. The latter often validates the former through empirical studies, making both disciplines cohere into a helpful and simple framework, detailing how, today, we can truly manifest peace. Religion and psychology—the latter relying on evidence-based techniques—will be shown to not only be compatible with one another, but, more often than not, will be saying the same thing. How they often supplement each other and support the findings of one another will be shown.

Though what follows draws on wisdom from all faith traditions, there is a preponderance of input from the Abrahamic faith traditions, specifically, the Christian traditions. However, that in no way precludes those outside the Abrahamic faiths from using the principles distilled here. Non-Abrahamic faith traditions add much wisdom to the pursuit of peace and are referred to in this work.

Internalizing the principles presented in this book can produce results that are nothing short of profound. Merely incorporating a few into our lives can be transformative and even curative.

One caveat is in order. It would be a mistake to assume that it is possible to maintain a state of constant peace, tranquility, or happiness. This would be unrealistic. Life does not work that way nor should it. In the fourth century of the Common Era, Saint Augustine famously said in his *Confessions* (probably the most popular book for Christendom after the Bible), "You have made us for yourself, O Lord, and our heart is restless until it rests in you."[1] This sentiment is very true, but some manner of peace can, in fact, be found this side of heaven in the here and now—a foretaste of the life to come, if you will. Granted, we cannot completely eradicate discord and disharmony in this life. This must be realized. However, peace is not elusive; we can, in all probability, have more of it than we presently have, but it does take some work and maintenance of the principles articulated here.

It should be noted at this point that our negative emotions actually serve a purpose. They let us know when something is wrong and in need of our attention Thus, they counterintuitively serve a positive purpose, calling for us to pay attention and address the issue, which may be internal or external. This work provides principles with which to address our internal states as well as external situations in order to reach a better emotional state and, thus, a healthier one which concomitantly allows for optimal functioning. Therefore, this book can be conceptualized as a road map for how to get back to a state of peace or closer to it than the place in which we currently find ourselves.

Many authors and spiritual giants inform the ideas explicated here and two are worthy of mention in light of the title of this work. Thich Nhat Hanh's book, *Being Peace,* and Thomas Keating's book, *Manifesting God,* are both packed full of insights, one from an Eastern perspective, Buddhism, and the other from a Western perspective, especially the Christian and Catholic tradition, respectively. The title of this book, at the very least, synthesizes the titles of these two great works and, undoubtedly, the pages that follow are informed by both these books and their respective traditions. It is hoped this short monograph, with its practical

1. Saint Augustine, *Saint Augustine,* 3.

techniques, informed by spiritual insights and the field of counseling and psychology, will help bring peace, healing, wholeness, tranquility, and contentment in life. It is, furthermore, hoped that this work will serve as a manual for life which you can return to often in order to help manifest peace in your life. The principles and pages that follow should go a long way in helping the reader with their personal journey towards manifesting peace.

Introduction

A RABBI ON SHALOM

IN THE FIRST CENTURY of the Common Era, a rabbi ascended a hilltop by the Sea of Galilee and spoke the now famous words known as the Sermon on the Mount. In delivering his discourse, Jesus of Nazareth uttered a sequence of Beatitudes. According to the Gospel of Matthew, Jesus spoke the following words to the gathered crowd: "Blessed are the peacemakers, for they will be called children of God" (Matt 5:9). Curiously, most people today do not stop to contemplate the meaning of these twelve words (eight in Greek, the language of the New Testament), for there is more to this utterance and the context in which it is found than most realize. There are profound implications in Jesus' words in this pronouncement. They are implications which, when unpacked and internalized, can bring healing and peace to our lives.

The context must first be properly understood. An ancient audience would have understood the significance of Jesus ascending atop a hill to deliver a message; we postmoderns likely fail to grasp this clue in the text. In the ancient Near East, for centuries it was understood that deities resided atop mountains or hilltops. There is even a tiny hill, measured in mere feet in Egypt, much smaller than the hills of Galilee, which was understood to be the residence of a deity. The Hebrew Bible and New Testament both also attest to this belief elsewhere.

In the Torah, Moses encounters God atop Mount Sinai, and Jesus, later in his ministry, is transformed into a radiant, glorious image on top of Mount Tabor. It is no coincidence these major events both occur on top of an elevated surface. The significance here is that deities are encountered on the same topographical feature as that upon which Jesus delivers his Galilean discourse where he explains the blessedness of being a peacemaker. The story, thus, presupposes that the deliverer of the message is, by virtue of where and how he delivers his message, a god. Those who understand Jesus to be divine, and even those who do not (but who still realize wisdom in his words), might want to pay close attention to what he is getting at in this short phrase about peacemakers.

That Jesus delivers this discourse on a hilltop just above the Sea of Galilee likely has significance as well, for an ancient motif existed of God's conquering the forces of chaos, which were often personified as the sea in ancient Near Eastern texts. This was the case for Marduk in the Babylonian epic, Enumma Elish, Canaanite literature for Baal, and even the Lord in the Hebrew Bible, particularly in Job, Isaiah, and the Psalms, as well as other Akkadian and Egyptian texts. It is little wonder that elsewhere in the Gospels, on more than one occasion, Jesus is portrayed as walking on the water of the Sea of Galilee as well as calming the storm on the same body of water—both portrayals imply a deity is present. More than just a miracle occurs in these instances; a divinity claim using an old motif is expressed, which is lost to modern readers, unfamiliar with the motif. This is all to suggest that there might be significance to the observation that when Jesus gives his discourse, he is standing atop a hill above the waters of the Sea of Galilee, as if to say: I, Jesus, stand above the forces of chaos and want to tell everyone about the importance and blessedness of peace and those who bring it. To bring it, we must have it, and how to obtain it is the purpose of this work.

Scholarship has also long noted how the Gospel of Matthew, where this short pronouncement regarding peacemakers is found, portrays Jesus in the image of Moses, while the Gospel of Luke seems to paint him more in the image of Elijah. Elsewhere, I have argued that it took all these images to begin to explain who this first century rabbi, who traversed ancient Palestine with a message of redemption and love, truly was.[2] Before explaining the significance of what Jesus is saying regarding peacemakers, we should first read his comment in its context:

> When Jesus saw the crowds, he went up the mountain; and after he sat down, his disciples came to him. 2 Then he began to speak, and taught them, saying: 3 "Blessed are the poor in spirit, for theirs is the kingdom of heaven. 4 Blessed are those who mourn, for they will be comforted. 5 Blessed are the meek, for they will inherit the earth. 6 Blessed are those who hunger and thirst for righteousness, for they will be filled. 7 Blessed are the merciful, for they will receive mercy. 8 Blessed are the pure in heart, for they will see God. 9 Blessed are the peacemakers, for they will be called children of God. 10 Blessed are those who are persecuted for righteousness' sake, for theirs is the kingdom of heaven. 11 Blessed are you when people revile you and persecute you and utter all kinds of evil against you falsely on my account. 12 Rejoice and be glad, for your reward is great in heaven, for in the same way they persecuted the prophets who were before you. 13 You are the salt of the earth; but if salt has lost its taste, how can its saltiness be restored? It is no longer good for anything, but is thrown out and trampled underfoot. 14 You are the light of the world. A city built on a hill cannot be hid. 15 No one after lighting a lamp puts it under the bushel basket, but on the lampstand, and it gives light to all in the house. 16 In the same way, let your light shine before others, so that they may see your good works and give glory to your Father in heaven. 17 Do not think that I have come to abolish the law or the prophets; I have come not to abolish but to fulfill." (Matt 5:1–17)

Brad Young's *Jesus the Jewish Theologian* explains that Jesus would have said these words in Aramaic, as his audience likely only understood this sister language to Hebrew. Thus, the word Jesus would have used for "peacemakers" in this text would have been a form

2. Anderson, *Extolling Yeshua.*

of the well-known Hebrew word "*shalom.*" The word "*shalom*" in Hebrew has a root meaning of "to make whole or complete." Thus, when Jesus says, "Blessed are the peacemakers," it is probably more apt to translate the meaning of his statement as "Blessed are those who make others whole or complete," or "Blessed are those who heal others." Though "peacemakers" is certainly not incorrect, the deeper meaning is "Blessed are healers." That is, blessed are those who heal others and help make others whole and complete. Individuals, such as therapists, medical personnel, healers of any type, and all of us—when we take the time to listen to or support a friend in need—are all acting in a manner that Jesus goes on to explain in the very next verse as worthy of the title "children of God." These jobs and endeavors attempt to bring *shalom* or peace to the lives of others. When we act in such a manner, we help bring *shalom* into the lives of others and the world. This, more often than not, also brings much peace to ourselves and makes us worthy of being called a child of God.

That *shalom* has taken on a meaning of peace in Hebrew, as well as become a greeting and farewell, perhaps obscures its wider original meaning. Its related Arabic cognate is *salaam*. Who has not traveled in the Middle East and been struck by the hospitality and beauty of the Muslim greeting, "*As-salāmu ʿalaykum,*" translated, "peace be upon you," or heard the common reply, "*waʿalaykum as-salām,*" translated, "and upon you, peace"? These phrases do demonstrate the innate human understanding of the significance and value of obtaining or having peace, and that such a state for a person is the most important thing one human could wish upon another. Expressing a desire that another have what is most important for their well-being shows that we hope the best for another, a sentiment in keeping with acting as a child of God.

Matthew 5:9 points to a reality—peace is foundational for our well-being. That is precisely why Jesus declares those blessed who help provide it for others. Its centrality to the well-being of humans is exactly why Jesus desires it for all. It is something we all so strive for and the absence of it is felt by all; its absence leads to much chaos in the world and in our individual lives and bodies.

This rabbi's words point to the primacy of peace because from it flows health, wholeness, clarity, understanding, compassion, and a better connection to God.

Elsewhere in the Gospels, Jesus explains, "Peace I leave with you; my peace I give to you. I do not give to you as the world gives. Do not let your hearts be troubled, and do not let them be afraid" (John 14:27). Thus, peace is an essential aspect in what this rabbi preached and being one of his followers provides. Possessing *shalom* or *salaam* is clearly good and beneficial and, according to this text, blessed are those who help bring it to others. This text presupposes that peace is precisely what people need. They need to be whole or complete. Thus, a monograph on the topic of how we can have more peace in this life is in order and is what follows.

In explaining that peacemakers are blessed, Jesus implicitly elevates the notion and importance, even sanctity, of peace. This needs to be understood and internalized and, when done, brings healing, wholeness, well-being, happiness, and health. The words of Jesus are a mandate for all to strive to be peacemakers. Before you can give peace to others, you must have it yourself. How to cultivate peace within yourself, which will, ultimately, lead to it exuding to others, is the purpose of this work. Said differently, the purpose of this book is to outline how to bring peace to you which, concomitantly, will bring peace to others. When you are at peace, it radiates to others, enacting the butterfly effect, and joy and peace often go hand-in-hand (see Rom 15:13). Conversely, the opposite is also true; for when you are not at peace, your discord or unease radiates to others as well. The absence of peace is corrosive and a very real, tangible problem for all. Life experience, no doubt, has proven this point to you. What follows lays out practices and techniques that will, undoubtedly, help readers bring a little more peace to their lives. Most, if not all, the principles articulated below are evidence-based and have much empirical support for their efficacy in bringing peace for individuals which creates peace for others and, ultimately, the world. Jesus specifically sanctifies and blesses those who bring peace in his Sermon on the Mount, delivered on a hilltop overlooking the Sea of Galilee. Peace starts with each of us and comes from within.

Introduction

PEACE TODAY AND OUR HEALTH

Virtually everyone desires more peace and happiness, but they seem to be more elusive in today's world, in which human beings can barely find the time to sit still and must constantly stay interconnected through social media with everyone they know, and often with people they do not know. We will not even address the issue of those who constantly post new photographs of themselves on social media outlets. Suffice it to say, this is a problem that is best saved for another book or article on narcissism. Most of us are inundated with a constant barrage of background, unnecessary noise. New data is coming out about how being more connected to email via our smart phones is causing more stress for people; data shows many often get up to send an email in the middle of the night.

Furthermore, some are calling the present era the "age of anger," with the economic and political unrest that can be felt merely by turning on the news, regardless of which news outlet. Perhaps that phrase is an apt one, as the climate does seem to be permeated with anger from every side, at the moment. Hence, the even greater need now for understanding and implementing the principles for finding peace delineated here. The techniques or principles are good for any age, person, persuasion, and culture, though different cultures will, no doubt, have nuanced understandings of the techniques here, as well as the members of the religious traditions quoted. This will be obvious when we come to the chapter on maintaining healthy boundaries. Having said that, anyone and everyone can adopt and benefit from the principles/ techniques explained here.

As noted in the foreword, long-term or sustained happiness is not a possibility. It is not possible or realistic to be in a constant state of happiness, nor should we desire such. Negative emotions serve a purpose; they often tell us something is wrong and, thus, must be attended to. However, negative emotions can be sinister, for when allowed to get the better of us, they can lead us from aggression to behavior that often lands us in trouble with the law, or worse, behind bars. They can also lead to disease in the body. Stopping them when they start is what is advanced here. Such behavior only manifests when we are not in a state of peace. If only nation states would also adopt the principles advocated here, as well as individuals, peace would surely reign. But it starts with individuals.

Therefore, we should strive not to linger too long in a negative emotional state. Though this almost goes without saying: returning to a state of peace or harmony is desired, when possible, for health reasons alone; negative emotional states, ultimately, have a detrimental impact on both mental and physical health. This is where this book and its principles come into play. They provide a means to get back on track and onto the road to peace and well-being. The aim of this work is to provide a blueprint for dealing with negative thoughts and emotions (which cause all our problems) and to manifest peace in our lives. In a way, this book can be thought of as a therapist in a book, distilling a holistic spiritual-type of therapy, taking the best from several disciplines.

The medical community has long known that peace is vital for well-being and studies show this much. The opposite of peace is discord and disharmony. The absence of peace can be felt when stress is present; therefore, we should pay attention for the telltale signs of it in our bodies and then take appropriate action. Appropriate action consists of checking in with the principles here and enacting the appropriate ones.

Extended periods of time under stress cause havoc to our bodies. In fact, some health care providers trace virtually all disease to it. Hence "dis-ease" is the problem. Stress is the result. Though stress is unavoidable in this life, peace is the antidote in order to achieve well-being and health. Stress is known to be positively correlated with disease (dis-ease). Hypertension and heart disease are but examples, which incidentally are the biggest killers in the West today. In fact, those who study stress estimate that it is the culprit for some 80 percent of all physical illnesses humans suffer. So, ways to combat stress and increase peace are vital, now more than ever, and the antidote is peace.

Remarkably, it has been shown that the level of a person's spirituality actually impacts mental health and well-being more so than a past trauma, such as abuse or a violent act, in a positive way. Thus, a work that aims to provide steps to engender peace in our lives, simultaneously combatting stress from a spiritual perspective and taking its insights and marching orders from the world religions and spiritual giants—past and present—is not only timely, but vitally needed at this juncture in human history.

We need to learn to get ourselves into a state of *shalom, salaam,* or a zen state, regardless of what is occurring around or outside us. We must cultivate a state of peace internally no matter what is occurring or will occur externally. Once attained, this internal tranquility oftentimes radiates and is contagious; it often even helps those around us calm down and achieve a sense of peace in the moment. We can then also serve as models for others. This peace comes from within, not from without, as is mistakenly presumed, often unconsciously. Undoubtedly, *shalom* can come from connecting with God, but it is still, largely, an internal connection. I have seen people who struggle immensely with anxiety disorders obtain *shalom* in spite of their predisposition toward anxiety—though notably, it takes effort and often continuously so, but it is well worth the effort. I doubt anyone would argue differently. The inward state of peace brings knowledge, not ostensibly intellectual, but more importantly, a peace felt at a deeper level in the heart which echoes the words of the great mystic, Julian of Norwich, who wrote, "in the end, all will be well."

The key to using the principles is to realize when you are not at peace and then to try to identify what is making you uneasy. First, you need to figure out how to self-soothe and get yourself from a negative emotional state to a more positive one. Second, work out how to rectify, if possible, the situation that made you not at ease or to figure out how to deal with it in a more productive, healthy manner in the future—assuming that is possible, as sometimes things that bring unease are not possible to avoid, at least in the short term.

Thus, and this is key, each of these techniques/principles offers a way out of negative emotions and negative states of mind. Make no mistake: negative emotional states such as anger, resentment, non-forgiveness, fear, and the like lead to unease and, eventually, disease. They wreak havoc on our bodies. These principles offer a way out, a way of getting yourself out of the mire of these negative states into positive, peaceful states of health. They can also offer ways to bring healing and stay out of the negative ways of being to which we, all too often, fall victim. These principles are a way to inward peace, stillness, and silence that does not allow all the trivialities of life to bother and disrupt our emotional well-being. You probably practice many of the principles below, but if you learn and implement only one of the principles below, it will likely bring much *shalom*. It cannot hurt to try.

TWELVE PRINCIPLES FOR MANIFESTING PEACE

It is not a coincidence that twelve principles have been chosen; twelve is a highly symbolic number in both the Hebrew Bible and the New Testament, just as forty and seven are. To be sure, its significance goes way back, even before the writing of the Bible. The significance of the number in the ancient Near East likely derives from the number of the gods in the pantheon and their respective, attributive planets, which both numbered twelve. It has taken on a sort of sanctity in the Bible because just as there were, symbolically, twelve tribes of Israel, so Jesus later in the Gospels, in a symbolic gesture, takes on twelve disciples, revealing an alignment with Israelite heritage. Just as we know, according to the Gospels, there were more than twelve disciples, there are more principles that could be added to the ones here. However, the disciples named and who have their journeys and work detailed in the Christian Bible and later traditions are the foundational disciples and so are the twelve principles provided in this work.

If you are like me, you like lists. They help simplify things. But this list of twelve principles is powerful for it contains principles informed by wisdom from the world's religions and has the power to transform a person's life, if implemented. Even taking on board one principle can have a life-changing effect for the better. These twelve principles can heal or just help us live a better, easier life, allowing for more fulfillment and happiness or joy.

As the first thing you probably did with this book was to go straight to the table of contents and read each principle, it likely became obvious how seemingly simple they appear. Upon reading each chapter, however, it will likely become just as apparent quite how profound each one can be, if adopted or increased in our lives. Furthermore, the profound wisdom of those spiritually inclined, such as Thomas Merton or Mahatma Gandhi, quoted in specific chapters, should come to the fore and give the reader a greater appreciation for each principle and how these mystics advocated and internalized the principles in their lives, and how this helped them manifest their own internal peace. Or perhaps this will occur in learning of the Hesychasts, those who practice inner stillness, silence, and calm among the monastics of the Orthodox tradition. It will be seen how their profound wisdom was put into action via a simple prayer repeated constantly and how we, too, can do the same.

The book always bears in mind God is the God of all people, regardless of religion or creed (Gal 3:28) and that wisdom can be found in any religious tradition or counseling and psychological school of thought. We are all his children and created in his image (Gen 1:27). Different traditions have different insights to offer on how to live the optimum life and obtain peace. They all have wisdom to teach and we can all learn from them without giving up the traditions to which we belong, or relinquishing the tenets to which we subscribe; doing so is not asked for in this book. Appropriating helpful insights and the principles that work best for you is suggested. It is to be noted that all the traditions here would likely maintain that God is a God of *shalom* or *salaam* and that true peace begins from within. It is also maintained here that any religious tradition would support, theologically, all of the principles that follow. How often can that be said!

UNIVERSAL RECOGNITION
OF PEACE BEING PARAMOUNT

That peace is the most desirable state a person can be in and can be wished for another can be seen in how tombstones are often marked, at least in the U.S. The sentiment or wish on tombstones "rest in peace" (R.I.P.) for those deceased, etched by loved ones, betrays the understanding that peace is the paramount or optimum state anyone can hope for another, especially those loved ones who will not be seen again this side of heaven. Two anecdotal stories from different traditions and eras are relevant and also show the primacy of peace. Siddhartha Gautama, before reaching an enlightened state and becoming the Buddha, left his family and home, renouncing all worldly desires and material things. Upon setting out on his path for enlightenment just after leaving his home, he was reported to have said he left in search of peace. Then, after six years of searching and trying different approaches, such as asceticism and ritual-type practices, he finally achieved enlightenment or awakening under the Bodhi tree. Buddha is then reported to have said: "I am at peace."

Peace is foundational for all religions and, really, psychology, too, as it implies or brings with it well-being and mental and physical health. Another Eastern religion, Jainism, emphasizes non-violence or Ahimsa as the first and last doctrine of the faith. This is their ethical precept and Jainism often has its adherents today meditate on the concept of peace for forty-five minutes to an hour a day, which reveals how much this tradition reveres peace.

There is a true story of a spiritually inclined man who sought guidance from his mentor, a holy Orthodox monk, who used to live on Mount Athos, known as Elder Paisios. He inquired regarding whether or not he should seek the life of a married man or a monastic Orthodox monk. Elder Paisios explained to the man, "You have to choose on your own what gives you peace." This very holy monk knew and, by his words, revealed that "peace" is the desired and necessary state for a person, regardless of the path they take or are on in this life.

Another Orthodox monk, Fr. Thaddeus, who ministered and counseled people in Serbia during tumultuous and brutal decades, often used to quote the words of St. Isaac the Syrian to those who came to him seeking guidance and advice: "Make peace with yourself and heaven and earth will make peace with you." Peace is, thus, at the heart of not only well-being, but what it means to live the best life we can. From it flows true health, well-being, and happiness, and the outflow of such a peace serves all of humanity in return.

As noted already, this work can be conceptualized as a therapist in a book. If you cannot afford a therapist or find a spiritual adviser, this book can serve as a substitute, as it draws from the wisdom of both domains and attempts to distill their most salient observations and methods that can be used for help in this life. One recommended use of this book is for a book club to read a chapter a week and discuss each principle when gathering: how each person has made use of the principle explained in a chapter in the past, or how the reader used it in the week prior to gathering. This can be helpful so others can be provided with tangible, real-life examples of these principles in action and hear about the specific results from people the reader knows. This can also help keep participants accountable and consistent with each principle for a time period, when trying them out.

The work can also be used piecemeal, that is, by the reader appropriating what works and discarding what does not. Some will jump to the chapter(s) they think will be helpful and skip others, which is fine. As the work draws from others in theology, religion, counseling, and psychology, it is hoped the book provides nuggets of wisdom gleaned from others that can be picked as desired and used to help obtain peace and radiate peace to others.

All too often, people make use of detrimental methods to cope with life's difficulties. People often self-soothe and run to that which, in the end, will not only suppress peace and cause other problems, but will also exacerbate current problems. Alcohol, drugs, smoking, promiscuous sex, overeating, undereating, cutting, and other risky behaviors are made use of to numb the pain or avoid and distract individuals from addressing issues. In the end, not only do these distractions create their own new problems, but they will not address the underlying issue; in fact, some of these, in the end, will not only destroy and lead to maladies, but will prevent the manifesting of true peace.

The avoidance of issues causes more problems, allows issues to continue, and decreases our quality of life. In the end, there are healthy and unhealthy coping methods people use to address issues. This book's principles can be conceptualized as healthy coping techniques that will, hopefully, become habits or second nature practices for lasting well-being. Coping with problems in unhealthy ways does more damage to a person more often than not. Therefore, addressing issues and learning ways to manage and cope in healthy adaptive ways is the key. Healthy coping methods, when practiced, become habits or default ways to deal with the negative emotions and problems. Learning to deal with issues more effectively and in a positive manner instead of utilizing harmful coping methods occurs when we make use of the principles below. This short work does not try to impress or be clever, but rather helpful. This short and concise work provides alternative, appropriate, and better-serving techniques than commonly used negative coping strategies to bring peace, healing, and a better life. It reveals how to tackle real issues head on with courage, drawing upon the insights of spirituality and evidence that has been brought to bear from the fields of counseling and psychology.

Every human being needs to make peace with others and for others, but, just as importantly, we need to make peace with ourselves and for ourselves. Thus, herein lies a blueprint or road map detailing very practical principles which, if adopted, will help bring true and lasting *shalom* and help us manifest peace.

Principle 1

Let Go of Caring
What Others Think of You

IF INCORPORATED INTO YOUR life, even to a small degree, this first principle can bring tremendous benefit to your well-being and sense of peace. It essentially maintains that you learn to adopt a posture, or attitude, of "so what?," in terms of caring about what others think of you. Admittedly, this takes practice, but it can be cultivated and, when internalized, peace will be realized within your being, a peace that has tremendous implications for your overall mental state. Too many know the feeling of walking around fretting that someone or a group thinks poorly of you. This can be incredibly debilitating and cause tremendous distraction with angst.

In reality, does it really matter what others think of you? And can you ever truly have everyone like you and think favorably of you? Are we always disposed to like everyone we meet? An affirmative answer to these questions is a definite impossibility. The truth is: not everyone is going to like you and that is OK. Some people will dislike you simply because of the color of your hair or how you look.

Often people will dislike you because you trigger something in the other person that reminds them of someone else they do not like: be it a family member, acquaintance, someone from the other person's childhood, or even something about themselves they dislike. This phenomenon also works in reverse in that we are often attracted to some people because, on a conscious or subconscious level, they remind us of someone else. Oftentimes, we are attracted to people because of unfinished business with a person from our childhood. Other people will trigger in us things we are not aware of that still need to be addressed. In psychological terms, this projection onto others of our own stuff, if you will, is called transference. Sigmund Freud recognized it and coined the term in the context of psychoanalysis and used it to treat his patients; harnessing this phenomenon in therapy is used today in psychodynamic therapy.[1]

This is all to say that individuals will dislike and like you because of a variety of factors that have nothing to do with you, factors out of your control. Thus, is it really logical to exert energy worrying about what others think of us when the outcome of being liked is out of our control, and the worrying does so much damage to us, in terms of robbing us of peace and well-being? We must realize it is impossible to please everyone and be liked by all. Thus, the principle of letting go of caring about what others think of you is a paramount principle for peace. Otherwise, you are seeking something impossible: to be liked by everyone all the time. That, in itself, is exhausting and anxiety provoking. Worrying about what others think sets you up for disappointment at some point. Why not give up the pursuit and just be yourself? Even if you succeed and perceive you are liked by another, there is often worry on the way to garnering that approval, followed by worry trying to keep it. Heaven forbid you lose that approval, which is likely to happen at some juncture, and which causes a real crisis when it happens to someone who puts too much emphasis on caring what others think of them.

1. See chapter 2 entitled "Psychoanalysis" in Murdock, *Theories of Counseling*, 29–64. See especially p. 51 on transference.

You have probably noticed that those over seventy in our culture very often tend to do a rather good job of adopting this attitude or principle, as they should. I suspect that, by this age, many realize the futility of wasting time and energy, not to mention creating angst, caring about what others think. Caring about what others think also causes people to act in ways contrary to who they really are and that is not a good thing. Doing so, in the end, will cause internal, cognitive dissonance and, therefore, should be avoided. This incongruity between what we believe and how we act will, in the end, cause a lot of internal strife and grief. Many therapists today see clients precisely when internal tension, due to this incongruity, reaches a level people can no longer tolerate. Often this is when people will make a change, as they should. The playwright and author, Oscar Wilde, said it best when he stated, "Be yourself; everyone else is taken." This is sound advice.

As you gradually relinquish the need for others to like you, you will let go of the need to impress others. The concern of being overly preoccupied with what others think of us is quite often an acute problem for those struggling with the different ways anxiety manifests itself in us—be it generalized anxiety, social anxiety, performance anxiety, panic attacks, and so forth. Cultivating this first principle alone can pay huge dividends in decreasing anxiety and, thus, increasing peace.

Religious traditions offer insights in regards to this principle. The famous prayer attributed to St. Francis of Assisi contains many pearls of wisdom and, specifically, one that pertains to this principle. The prayer begins by imploring the Lord to make the supplicant a vessel of peace. The first half, essentially, asks that where negative, harmful emotions exist, the petitioner may replace these with positive, pure and godly opposites. The latter half consists of asking God to work on the petitioner that we may not seek things for ourselves, but rather cultivate certain desirable things for others which we would, normally, ask for ourselves. Its beauty can be seen on every line. It reads:

> Lord, make me an instrument of your peace. Where there is hatred, let me sow love; Where there is injury,

pardon; Where there is doubt, faith; Where there is despair, hope; Where there is darkness, light; Where there is sadness, joy.

O Divine Master, grant that I may not so much seek to be consoled as to console, to be understood as to understand, to be loved as to love; for it is in giving that we receive; it is in pardoning that we are pardoned; it is in dying to self that we are born to eternal life [2]

One sentiment in particular brings to the fore an important aspect of this principle. Namely, "O Divine Master, grant that I may not so much seek . . . to be understood as to understand." Essentially, this sentiment can help us realize that it does not matter what others think of us, but rather that we have a proper understanding of a situation and what is going on for someone else. It does not hurt to think of this and repeat this phrase to ourselves at times when we realize that our anxiety or upset mood is the product of caring too much about what others think of us. I have personally seen this specific technique bring benefit to people in counseling. Furthermore, when we feel that another person dislikes us or thinks of us in a negative manner, we should recall the words of Jesus at the end of the Beatitudes in the Sermon on the Mount: "Blessed are you when people revile you and persecute you and utter all kinds of evil against you falsely on my account. Rejoice and be glad, for your reward is great in heaven, for in the same way they persecuted the prophets who were before you" (Matt 5:11–12). This gives us a real chance to put faith into practice and suggests we are doing something right, aligning us with those ancient exemplars of the faith.

Buddhism also has much to teach with regard to this principle of letting go. One of its main tenets extols us to relinquish desire, or, more accurately, to seek to temper desire and cravings. This wisdom is applicable because caring what others think of you is really, at its core, a *desire* that the other person(s) think of you in a positive manner. If you let go of the need or desire to be liked, as well as other misplaced and frivolous desires, such as the need to

---

2. Cook, *Francis of Assisi*, 125.

be the most popular or have the most money and power, or to be perceived of as the smartest person in the room and so forth, life can be enjoyed so much more and it can be immensely freeing. It is important to note that this tenet of Buddhism is compatible with Christianity and other faith traditions. Monastic practitioners in many of the different faith traditions exemplify this.

It is not suggested here that it will not take hard work to get to a place where you can, honestly, say you have given up the need or desire for others to like you, but it is possible. You can, at least, give up the need to some degree and experience real relief and healing, even without completely giving up the desire altogether. Only partially enacting this principle can be tremendously helpful. I write from experience. You can also enlist another principle to help with this one: watching your thoughts, which is largely influenced by cognitive behavioral therapy.

Remember that you cannot control what others really think of you and it is absolutely impossible to have everyone like you. This is simply part of the human condition. Therefore, you need only realize when this desire/way of thinking, or its by-products of unease and anxiety, are present in your body and remind yourself that it *truly* does not matter. What matters is where we stand in relationship to God. Also, in our busy world, it is always important to remember to relax and breathe and not to be so hard on yourself (see Rom 3:23). You need not always take life or yourself so seriously. We, all too often, forget to try and enjoy this gift of life, often because we are too preoccupied exerting needless energy worrying about what others think of us. The worry never affects the outcome and causes havoc in our bodies. Peace comes when we make a conscious effort to adopt the "let go of caring what others think of you" principle. After appropriating this principle, no doubt with some effort and practice (especially with the help of watching and altering your thoughts, described further on as Principle 8), you will truly experience a manifesting of peace.

Principle 2

Let Go of the Need to Be Right

PROVERBS 21:2 READS, "EVERY way of a man is right in his own eyes, but the Lord weighs the hearts." Could this ancient verse from a wisdom text be more true? It is human nature to always labor under the assumption that we are right and, as a consequence, someone else, or even, everyone else, is wrong. Oftentimes, we likely are right, but clinging to the need to be right, irrespective of whether or not we are, causes problems in relationships and for our internal peace.

If you are like me, you are probably reading this and immediately thinking, "If only my partner or (especially) ex could have adopted such a view." Therein lies an insight: just as you are thinking of another person negatively in their inability to admit when the other was wrong or inability to let go of the need to be right, so others view you in the same manner when you cannot let go of the need to be right. This reveals how not enacting this principle damages relationships. The sterner we are on this score, and the longer we engage the world without consideration of this principle, the more damage is done and the less likely it is we have many quality-filled relationships.

We lack much internal peace when we need to be correct and prove another wrong all the time. Angst is further built up internally when we feel we must win another over to our point of view, which is rarely possible, especially when we want to change another's belief. Beliefs go deeper than thoughts and are connected with emotions, so even logic, at times, will not change a person's perspective. Religious and political beliefs are prime examples, and demonstrate how even the use of sound logic often does not change a person's core beliefs.

Marriages often suffer immensely because one or both partners lack the ability to enact this principle. Any married person can attest to that fact. When one partner has to prove themselves right it causes many problems, often exacerbating a relatively minor disagreement and growing it into a greater problem. Though not the problem originally, it can become a contributing factor in a problem continuing and then causing much bigger issues. If one learns to divorce emotions and the need to be right when both parties in a relationship do not see eye-to-eye, a genuine healing occurs and the relationship can flow more harmoniously.

Jainism, an ancient religion from India, understands that we can never be completely right about a matter. The faith argues there is no absolute truth and argues against all forms of absolutism, though this, in itself, might ironically be a form of absolutism.[1] Jainism uses a story to illustrate this point, a tale also used in other Eastern religions. The gist of the story goes that a group of blind men is taken to examine an elephant. Each man holds a different part of the elephant: the leg, ear, tusk and so forth. Afterwards, each describes what an elephant is. Each correctly describes what they felt and describes the elephant; however, because of the different parts of the body the blind men describe, they only explain the elephant in part. This tale captures the truth that you can only describe something from your perspective, from what you glean, which is always limited. The men were blind and could only describe their specific portion of the elephant. What each said was true, but only in part and from their perspective. This is reminiscent of 1 Corinthians 13:12: "For now we see in a mirror, dimly, but then we will see face to face. Now I know only in part; then

1. Matthews, *World Religions*, 178–89.

I will know fully, even as I have been fully known." Thus, none of us ever has all the information and, in reality, we should never presume we are always correct, for then we are lacking humility and presuming to be God. A certain amount of humility is called for in this life and all religious traditions espouse its importance.

Jains understand that no one has a monopoly on truth, as we all see things from a different perspective. This is illuminating. The New Testament, essentially, says the same thing in the context of the life to come, quoted above from 1 Corinthians 13:12. This is an important insight, made by both traditions, to keep in mind, especially when arguing with someone. In reality, no one has all the facts.

To be honest, most of us fail to enact this principle, in part, because of our own stubborn pride, something that all too often gets in the way. Pride is a universal, insidious problem that has, perhaps, done more damage to the world than anything else. Wars have begun because of it and whole groups have been slaughtered because of it. In fact, Saint Augustine, in the fourth century, wisely said that all sin is pride. The problem is that individuals quite often think they are the center of the universe. A work from an unknown author written around the middle of the fourteenth century, and revered by Martin Luther, *Theologia Germanica*, offers an intriguing interpretation of the so-called fall and what it was that Adam did, a view that offers humanity an important message: "This assumption and his 'I' and his 'me' and his 'mine'—that was his apostasy and his fall." It continues, "What else did Adam do than precisely this thing? We are used to saying that Adam was lost and fell because he ate that apple. I say it was because of his presumption and because of his I and his Mine, his Me and the like."[2] The point the author is making is related to the issue of our pride, our sense of entitlement. Along this line of thought, needing to be right is like being entitled. This need falls in line with our pride. We cannot be wrong or our pride will be injured. Giving up the need to be right is, in large measure, working on keeping our pride in check—the root of so many of our problems, so much

2. Luther, *Theologia Germanica*, 62.

so it was even counted as one of the so-called seven deadly sins. Cultivating some measure of humility is, thus, called for to help enact this principle of letting go of the need to be right. It should be noted humility does not presuppose self-deprecation. Many a humble person still values themselves appropriately.

The remedy to the problem of needing to always be right is for us to adopt a proper view that understands: it is not all about me. Everyone, from time to time, needs to tell themselves this. Thomas Merton offers a corrective, alternative way of thinking that runs counter to humanity's often default way of thinking and acting, too often driven by pride: "Clean, unselfish love does not live on what it gets, but on what it gives. It increases by pouring itself out for others, grows by self-sacrifice and becomes mighty by throwing itself away."[3] He says we should act out of love, rather than pride, and that love grows by being given away and that is true loving. Thus, it is not about me, rather it is about helping others. We are all interconnected and all God's children. Eastern religious traditions go so far as to say that not only are we connected to another, but, in some way, the other is us. Thomas Merton was very much intrigued with Eastern spirituality.

Thus, when we realize it is not all about us, and we have a proper perspective, in terms of our ego, we will easily be able to adopt and enact the principle of letting go of the ridiculous need to be right. How better the world would be if people could only admit when they are wrong, for no one is ever always right. There is a personality disorder, which is chiefly characterized by an inability to admit when one is wrong, showing how problematic this inability is. We too often strive to be right and stop listening to and caring for others. Our ego gets hurt and then we need to prove its worth.

Anyone who has adopted this principle, even in part, can recall a time when they were able to admit being wrong, though it was likely hard at first, and some measure of anger likely had to be quelled internally. As you go about your day, look to see where you might be wrong and where you might need to implement this

3. Merton, Waters of Siloe, xviii.

principle, for it is doubtful you are always right—only God is. If you never admit you are wrong (and you surely know if this is the case on some level), you might consider working on this principle. Relief and peace come when we enact this principle, and set ourselves free from the need to always be right. It brings a sort of freedom, which is a by-product of peace, not to mention a dramatic ease in virtually all interpersonal relationships.

Principle 3

Refrain from Assumptions

In *The Four Agreements*, Don Miguel Ruiz draws from Toltec wisdom and notes how humans have a tendency not only to make assumptions, but then to believe they are the gospel truth. We, curiously, and perhaps humorously, believe we are mind readers. Elsewhere in his work, he explains the need to seek clarification and not to attempt to be a mind reader. This is wise counsel for all and, thus, principle number three of this work.

As far as the present author is aware, no person has ever been able to read minds. Proceeding as though we can, albeit often just beneath our consciousness, often gets us into trouble. Frequently, we assume someone else is thinking about us maliciously or has some nefarious agenda, which, consequently, evokes a negative response on the mind-reader's part, which creates a negative response in the person who is supposedly having their mind read, thus creating a disharmonious, vicious cycle. An entire course of action can often be driven by incorrect assumptions regarding what we think someone else is thinking. We are frequently wrong regarding what someone else is thinking and we, as noted already, rarely, if ever, have all the facts. It is best, therefore, not to make assumptions.

In presuming to know what others are thinking, we are often wrong and harbor incorrect assumptions, which then drive our thoughts and actions and affect our emotions. This simple mistake has a domino effect, bearing on virtually every aspect of our lives. Regrettably, experience has likely taught the reader that, often, our views with regard to what others are thinking tend toward the cynical and negative. Data has also shown this to be the case most often when we think about ourselves, which will be addressed later in this book. Humans are, thus, being hijacked and directed away from peace because of erroneous assumptions made as a result of attempts to mind read. Therefore, again, it is best simply not to make assumptions.

This principle is particularly helpful in romantic relationships and marriages. Marriage counselors frequently have clients engage in asking what each client is thinking when both are together. Often, simply through one partner in the relationship just listening to what their spouse/partner is sharing, enlightenment comes to the listening party, fostering empathy and understanding. This, in turn, helps the other person feel heard and allows the one listening to realize that they did not truly know what their partner was thinking. This also helps to foster a more positive communication pattern. In a way, this also demonstrates one of the unspoken rules in mental health counseling that, by building empathy and understanding, the client only needs realizations and insights in therapy and, consequently, they can see what is going on in their life and will then know what is best for them in their specific situation.

Therefore, we should never assume to know exactly what another's thoughts and motives are. We never truly know what another is going through or has been through. We never know what someone else might be carrying with them from their childhood that might be causing them to act in a certain manner in the present. Just as we want God's grace and understanding, so, too, should we show others the same. Thus, principle three "not making assumptions" is vital for our peace, as well as that of others.

PRINCIPLE 4

Suspend All Judgment
and Let Others Live Their Lives

THIS PRINCIPLE IS A particularly difficult one to internalize because, on a primal level, judging others serves a purpose: it protects
us. Humans need to be able to judge when danger is present and
react accordingly. Perhaps the qualification of "generally speaking"
should be added to this principle, for we cannot completely relinquish judging others and, for obvious reasons, nor should we seek
to completely stop doing so. However, too much judging of others
is problematic and should be tempered. In so doing, much peace
will be manifested.

This principle not only applies to judging others, but also
to judging ourselves. Guilt and self-deprecation wreak havoc on
our physical and mental well-being, and both are the product of
judging ourselves, all too often, too harshly. We should recall the
words Paul wrote to the church in Rome: "All have sinned and fall
short of the glory of God" (Rom 3:23). If God forgives you, and
God does, then why should you not forgive yourself? Do you think
you know better than God? To such corrosive, detrimental introspection, brought about by judging ourselves too harshly, we need
remember that we are all children of God, made in his image (Gen

1:27) and therefore worthy. We need also bear in mind that God forgives every sin.

Recall the great figures of the Bible and the sins they committed: David murdered Uriah the Hittite because he wanted his wife and likely forced himself on Bathsheba; Moses murdered an Egyptian in his anger; and Saul, later known as Paul, was culpable in the death of Stephen, as recounted in the book of Acts. If these paradigmatic figures, who were incredibly fallible men, were chosen by God, forgiven, and used to enact God's purposes in the world, so too are you forgiven of your mistakes and missteps, no matter how grave or heinous. We, therefore, need not be so hard on ourselves. We, too often, judge ourselves more harshly than God judges us.

Judging others more than is needed to survive and function properly in the world is, and has been, an acute problem for humanity since the beginning, so much so that several biblical injunctions against doing so are recorded in the Bible and in the very words of Jesus: "Do not judge, and you will not be judged" (Luke 6:37); "Or how can you say to your neighbor, 'Let me take the speck out of your eye,' while the log is in your own eye?" (Matt 7:4)

The story of the woman caught in adultery in John 8 makes a similar point. Whoever is free from sin should be the one to cast the first stone. Not surprisingly, no stone is thrown and the woman escapes unhurt. The proverbial saying, "People who live in glass houses should not throw stones," rings true. We all, ultimately, live in glass houses. Thus, no one has the right to judge another, for we all have too many issues in which we "miss the mark" (the literal translation the Hebrew word for sin, חטה). The Bible makes it clear we should not exert time or energy focusing on the faults of others, nor should we engage in gossip regarding the faults and shortcomings of other people.

A children's saying is applicable here: when you point your finger at someone, you are really pointing three back at yourself. It is pithy, though apt. How you judge someone else really tells more about you. What psychologists designate as "mirror effect" is that you can only love or hate in another what you yourself possess. You dislike something about someone else because you see that trait or attribute in yourself and do not like it. Thus, the "mirror effect" maintains you can only love or hate in someone else what you possess and love or hate about yourself. The implication is that what you say about someone else is really a commentary about yourself. Being cognizant of this phenomenon is important and will likely help temper your judgment against others or help give you pause before being critical of another. The Golden Rule is applicable here, as if we do not want others to judge us, so we should not judge others. More on the Golden Rule later, but, also, suffice it to say, anyone can find fault with anyone, for we are all human and fault can always be found in all of us, if you merely have a cursory look. It is best not to judge for we desire not to be judged.

This principle, therefore, calls for letting other people live their own lives. People need to make their own mistakes and learn their own lessons from them. Oftentimes, in trying to help another person after we have judged them or their actions, we fall into the trap of trying to save them and commit the "sin" of offering unsolicited advice—something virtually everyone does not appreciate or desire. This often occurs when a person surmises someone is going in the wrong direction, in their estimation, and, out of love or kindness, wants to help. This is not to say speaking your truth or piece of mind to someone is not to be done, though it rarely helps. Additionally, if someone is putting themselves in grave danger or imminent harm, by all means, we need to intervene; however, this is rarely the case and more often the exception. Remember, people do not want unsolicited advice. And when they ask for it, they usually just want you to agree with them.

Remember you can, in most cases, only change yourself and how you react to someone or a situation, not another person. However, this axiom does not hold for the raising of children when they are young, but it will for when they are older, a point many parents later struggle with, as they often want to control and direct the lives of their children. Two points on this score are in order. Parents have children to give them life, not to live life through them, as a client once realized in a therapy session I was in. A parent does well to remember this after kids leave the nest, so to speak. Secondly, if you notice yourself, as a parent, falling into the trap of needing to control everything in your kid or in anyone else and even your own life, this might be a sign of anxiety that needs to be addressed with another principle in this book, specifically, "catching and altering your thoughts." Just as anger is often how depression manifests itself, so too the need to control is how anxiety often manifests itself. This is just something to look for in yourself and be aware of. Of course, you can also be proactive and take action with the principles in this book, when needed. The comments here about control are in line with another principle that will be articulated later on: maintaining healthy boundaries. This current principle dovetails nicely with that one, as they go together. Thus, we cannot change what other people do, but we can change our reactions to them/it. A war, quite literally, can be waging outside of ourselves while we can be at complete peace inside ourselves. There are many stories of spiritual individuals from across the spectrum of religious traditions achieving this level of peace, even in the midst of tumultuous and life-threatening situations. This level of peace is possible.

The Eastern religion of Jainism is informative in regards to not judging others and letting things be as they are. Many of the monastic traditions in this faith have their monks spend their lives walking and spreading a message of peace through non-violence. As part of this, they attempt to cultivate an attitude of letting things be, which seems to coincide with a state of peace. You let others live their lives, thus releasing worry and manifesting more peace for self, which always flows to others. Naturally, we cannot always do this, as we have a duty to intervene for the safety and health of others, to protect someone on occasion, but, again, this is usually not the norm. Normally, it is best, for the sake of peace, to let others simply be or let others live their own lives.

With regards to not judging ourselves, the practice of mindfulness, which will be more fully articulated later, needs to be mentioned here. Mindfulness practice involves noticing and observing ourselves and our surroundings and, by extension, can be used to see what is occurring in others. However, mindfulness practice, which also grows out of Eastern religious traditions, maintains as one of its main principles that we do not judge even the negative emotions or thoughts we have. That has very big implications. We can use mindfulness practice to notice others, but not judge what we see. Thus, you do not suppress what is seen in others and then in yourself, including your reactions to others and situations; you simply acknowledge them. This is insightful and informative for how to live life in regards to not judging what you see in others or yourself. You accept things without judgment, which brings a sort of freedom and realness.

I have seen this mindfulness work in conjunction with relying on one's faith to help heal those who have been sexually abused. More on this mindfulness approach below, as it is helpful when anxiety and guilt arise in our minds: rather than suppressing such negative thoughts, they are acknowledged, but not judged— neither the thought, nor the person.

Another problem with judging needs to be mentioned. Humans tend to mimic other people, usually subconsciously. You can see this by simply observing individuals. Often, when someone rubs their nose or scratches their head, within a few seconds, the other person will do the same. We know from studies that people can pick up on the emotional states of others subconsciously. For example, a study found that we have a heartbeat between our heartbeats that betrays our emotional state. When spending time with someone, our beat between a heartbeat will pick up on another person's and start to mimic it. This can be seen in the documentary *I am,* which addresses the phenomenon in more detail. Thus, when we judge people, often subconsciously, another can pick up on our judgmental attitude toward them. We do not even consciously realize that we often also put out cues that are subconsciously picked up on by others. We, therefore, put out negative vibes, quite literally, that are picked up on. At this point, our peace is affected and so is the peace of another person. This vibe is almost always sent back to us by the other person when they are judged and then they judge us for having judged them and, thus, the negative cycle continues, not to mention the impact judging has on the relationship between the two people. I can attest that my judging of another person led to the destruction of a relationship. Words have never been exchanged about it, but I know my judgmental attitude was picked up on by the other person and the energy was transmitted back to me, thus ruining a relationship. This is one real example of how judging others is corrosive and does much harm to the peace of the judge and those being judged.

Why not choose to stop the cycle that disrupts peace in its tracks by not judging? If you are being judged and you enact principle one by letting go of caring whether someone else likes you or what others think of you, you stop the cycle for both you and the other person, thus manifesting peace for yourself, others, and even the world. The peace of the world can be affected because negative cycles are perpetuated on even grander scales between people, groups, and countries. Wars thus ensue. If you desire to change the world, start with yourself and those around you and stop judging. This is something you, actually, have the literal power to do. Judging leads to hate. Stop the cycle in its tracks and, literally, change the world. A long journey starts with one step, as they say. Here, you are taking one step for the world and others to manifest peace in the world. This is how everyone can contribute to making the world a better place: each person taking one step.

This being the case, cultivating an attitude of "radical non-judgment" of self and others is suggested. I have actually prescribed this to a few clients and they have reported tremendous results after adopting this posture and putting it into practice. I, specifically, directed several clients to practice "radical non-judgment" of others and self between one session and the next. The practice paid huge dividends for these clients' well-being and peace. In the end, such a posture is really simply obeying the commandment of Christ of not judging. What follows from it is peace: peace with oneself and others. This, in turn, helps radiate peace to the world. This is one way we can manifest peace for ourselves and for humanity as well as all of creation.

Principle 5

Maintain Healthy Boundaries

PEACE IS FOUND WITHIN, not in someone else. That it is to be found in someone else is a common misconception and mistake people make in relationships. People often surmise happiness or peace will come from someone else when in reality we must find peace and happiness within ourselves, whether we are alone or in a relationship. It is a recipe for disaster to look for it in someone else. We have to be happy with ourselves. It is a mistake to think a partner will bring it.

One of the fastest ways to diminish peace is to engage in unhealthy boundaries. If you do, you end up giving your power away, which makes your happiness and peace contingent on the situation with the other person. In the end, you can only control your own emotions and well-being, not anyone else's, nor should you try. Doing so creates an unhealthy boundary. With regard to relationships, a healthy boundary includes not worrying about someone else's problems. You really should only pray for another and model the behavior you want to see. As Mahatma Gandhi stated, we should be the change we want to see in the world. Be what you want to see. This might manifest what you desire, but be cautious with your desires, for they can manifest an unhealthy boundary.

These truths arise out of structural family systems theory used in marriage and family therapy, as opposed to strategic family systems theory that seeks to address and target specific issues with strategic interventions. Structural family systems theory and therapy addresses the overall structure of the family system that enables how it functions. Both structural and strategic are helpful, but the former is particularly helpful with regard to how families and boundaries among family members work. It is often helpful to correct the boundaries between family members when they are either too porous or too inflexible. As with virtually everything else in life, balance or equilibrium is needed.

Granted, the level of how porous or how rigid a boundary should be is subjective and culturally conditioned. For example, it is important to note Mediterranean and Hispanic families think more in terms of a group, family unit than an Anglo-Saxon family, which often thinks more in terms of autonomy or values individuality more. I see this issue in my own family with it being a mix of Hispanic and White/Anglo, hence a typical American family in many respects.

What is deemed to be an enmeshed family, to use the parlance of systems theory, might not seem as enmeshed to someone from another culture. This is all to suggest people will have a difference of opinion here based on their values and their culture, which is fine. This is still a healthy principle and balance should be sought based on your personal values, culture, and what feels right for you. The reader is the best judge and knows what is right for them. Perhaps the phrase "generally speaking" is appropriate here again. However, no boundaries are a problem and too rigid of boundaries are problematic, too, so some measure of balance is requisite for all, to be sure. It is important to strike the balance for what works for you and brings you peace. You likely already inherently know if you need a tweaking of your boundaries in order to have healthier ones that bring you more peace. This notion is to be applied to all relationships, be they family, friends, or work-related.

Not putting up a healthy boundary with someone who takes advantage of you in any way, whether it be your time or monetary help, can cause disharmony and unease, while having too rigid of a boundary with a child or loved one might cause you to miss out on loving relationships, hurt a loved one, or miss out on the grace of God and blessings others give you in this life. In each case, your peace is forfeited, even in the second example, as, on some level, you might be ill at ease knowing you are missing out on God's grace and missing out on giving yourself over in love to a friend, a call of all religious traditions. It is a balancing act because, at the same time, you only have so much to give and do not want to be walked on or taken advantage of. This also robs you of having the energy to give yourself to others and, ironically, not only hurts you yourself, but others, too.

Balance is key; listen to your intuition and body on this score. If you lack peace in the context of a relationship, that is a sure sign there might be an unhealthy boundary present. Listen to your body; it will tell you if peace is lacking. Are you annoyed with a person or anxious because they are being allowed to continue to cross or transgress your boundaries? Do not give your power away. Establish or reestablish a healthy boundary. This can be done in a polite, though firm way, and should be respected by a friend. If it is not respected, you need to decide whether that person is truly a friend or someone using you and zapping your energy without giving anything back. Sometimes, when someone takes your energy repeatedly, it is suggestive of a person with a problematic ego or even a personality disorder, which does not mean you abandon your friend, but rather you be cautions and evaluate the relationship. I would never advocate cutting someone out of your life just because they crossed boundaries, or not forgiving someone who has wronged you and even continues to do so unabashedly. However, you might need to reevaluate how much time you spend with them if they do not show you the respect you need to maintain a healthy boundary and manifest serenity and peace. Most people will want the best for you and thus respect your boundaries—so long as they truly understand the situation, which often needs to be gently explained to them.

Those of Mediterranean and Hispanic cultures, among others, are not as used to this approach and, consequently, might actually find it immensely helpful. Numerous times I have witnessed people obtain more peace in their lives remarkably rapidly after implementing healthy boundaries in their relationships.

A healthy boundary consists also of simply realizing and proceeding from the understanding that I am in charge of my own emotions and control my emotions, thoughts and behavior, not someone else. It means proceeding from the understanding that my happiness or any other emotion is not contingent on someone else, but on myself. I control my peace. Now, granted, this is not always the case, but the vast majority of the time it is. The internalizing and acting out of such an understanding can have profound implications for our level of peace and self-sufficiency as well.

As stated several times already, we can only control ourselves, not someone else, so we need to learn to let go and let others live their lives, for this allows healthy boundaries. We only need live our own lives. As said previously, I once heard a mother say, after years of therapy struggling with control issues related to her daughters, that she finally realized she did not have a child to live her own life through, but gave her child life in order for her child to live it. What an insight from which a healthy boundary arose.

The emphasis on creating healthy boundaries is not to suggest, as faith traditions explain, that we are to refrain from helping and taking care of others. To some degree, we are our brother's keeper, as the story of Cain and Abel suggests (Gen 4:9). This is true when appropriate, while sometimes helping others help themselves and build autonomy is part of the help we can provide another. As the proverbial saying goes, it is better to teach a person to fish than to give fish to a person. Granted, there is a healthy middle ground between providing help and enabling a person, as there is between having a healthy boundary and a lack of one. Having a healthy boundary and being discerning, on a case-by-case basis, will allow us to know when help is genuinely needed and when a boundary must be maintained. Listening to our intuition or the Spirit within can be helpful on this score. Albeit, sometimes things will be ambiguous, but if they are continually ambiguous, this might suggest an unhealthy boundary is present or you are being taken advantage of, or that you need to help yourself instead of continuing to rely on another's assistance.

Most societies tend to emphasize the collective more than the individual. Hispanics families place more value on the family and tend to think more in terms of the group than Anglos who think more in terms of the individual, as noted above. This plays out in multiple ways: one being boundaries with kids. A Hispanic family often allows the children to sleep in the same bed as the parents, whereas this is often deemed unacceptable in Anglo households. Real differences exist in regard to boundaries. This must be realized before judging one as right and the other as wrong. Having issued that caveat, a healthy balance is needed between communal thinking and the individual. Both are important. Maintaining healthy boundaries can be highly effective for the well-being of both families and individuals. All can profitably benefit from adopting this principle of incorporating healthy boundaries in relationships.

Maintaining healthy boundaries is requisite for maintaining peace in our lives, but it is important to bear in mind that culture will play a role with regard to the extent or rigidity of the boundaries. And what constitutes a healthy boundary for you will differ from someone else. Although cultural conditioning has a bearing, it is safe to say that an unhealthy boundary is one, irrespective of culture, when it causes discord and disturbs our peace. This is an important point. Thus, the telltale sign of an issue with boundaries that likely needs your attention is when you do not have peace or are causing someone else not to have peace. This suggests a boundary has been crossed. This is the measurement to be used, namely, when peace is disturbed.

To some extent, this coincides with principle 4, regarding letting others live their lives. You cross a boundary when you try to impart or subject your desires and thinking onto someone else, or when you attempt to have someone else conform to the way you think things need to be in a relationship. We often do need to do a better job of letting others live their lives and keeping an appropriate boundary for ourselves as well as others. If someone is about to do something that will bring them harm, we need to step up and say something to them. Applying reason and logic to all these principles is important, for they are not absolute. Anything that is absolute must be examined because absolute positions are dangerous. A caveat should be stated again at this point: most of the principles argued for here should be qualified with "generally speaking." Having said that, we need to allow for others to have autonomy and live their lives. We need to respect people.

Healthy boundaries often relate to the issue of triangles. Murray Bowen's work on family systems demonstrated that, often, when conflicts arise in families, and, really, in any relationship, a third party is pulled in and triangulated, as people generally want to bring others to their side of an issue.[1] Thus, a problem exists when a triangle is present. The model suggests that, when we find ourselves in a triangle in life, we need to do what we can to get out of the triangle. I would argue implementing a healthy boundary is usually the way out. In a problem or conflict, you are one of the three, represented by the corners of a triangle. You are either the aggressor, the victim, or the rescuer. This model is not all that different from the model used to describe co-dependency. Individuals often move from one position in a triangle to another, from an aggressor to a victim and back, for example. Personality types obviously come into play here. So, if you are an aggressor, you to need stop and get out of the triangle as this wrecks peoples' peace and well-being, including your own. If you are a victim, you often need to erect a healthy boundary to get out of the triangle or learn to find your voice and say "no" or "stop" to another. You may need to learn how to stop letting others turn your "no" into a "yes." When that happens, you end up doing something you do not want to do and ultimately you will become resentful and angry, thus, not at peace. Finally, being a rescuer can result in internalizing other's problems and becoming overwhelmed, often to the point of becoming sick. The rescuer also does not allow victims to develop their own autonomy. Being a rescuer and wanting to fix everyone's

1. Kerr and Bowen, *Family Evaluation*, 134.

problems takes a large toll on a person, eventually. Thus, when we find ourselves in a triangle in life, we need do what it takes and get out in a healthy and respectful way as soon as possible. Erecting healthy boundaries is often the most appropriate way to get out of the triangle. When we do that, peace is attainable.

Here is an example: A mother and daughter are fighting and the daughter calls her brother to complain about the mother. The daughter is attempting to triangulate. A healthy boundary and response is for the brother to say, "I am sorry about your conflict, but I know the two of you can work it out, so I am staying out of it. So, let's talk about something else." The brother has not allowed himself to become the rescuer and become sucked into the triangle. He has erected a healthy boundary. Another example is a high-school student bullied at school and always running to a friend for help. In this case a healthy way out of the triangle for the victim, the one being bullied, is to tell the aggressor(s), if it is safe to do so in their case, that they need to stop or they will be reported to the administration. The victim finds his voice in this case. If the aggressor(s) continues, the student (victim) then reports the aggressor, the bully, and stands up for themselves, thus self-advocating. The victim builds autonomy by not relying on a rescuer, his friend in this case, and steps out of the triangle. The key for this case is for the student not to step back in later and take on a different role, such as being a bully or aggressor, which often occurs, as those who bully often were bullied, just as those who abuse were often themselves abused previously. The cycle needs to be stopped. People need to be their own person and step outside of triangles when they find themselves in them. Peace thus ensues. These are but two of thousands of examples.

With regard to healthy boundaries, it is important to remember that it is virtually never possible to agree with someone on everything. Thinking that could happen is an unrealistic, harmful expectation. In fact, agreeing with someone on everything would, ultimately, be boring. Recall the joke of two rabbis in a room and, consequently, there will be three opinions. Yes, everyone has one, as the joke goes.

History has taught us that any push or attempt at uniformity of belief will usually cause violence to ensue. So, let people live their lives and do not try to change their opinions—maintain a healthy boundary. When you realize the importance of this understanding, you will be more at peace in realizing you cannot agree on everything and will be able to let it go. This will reduce the frustration that is likely to arise when others do not agree with you. In a roundabout way, this will also help release the need for others to like you. It is best to give it up and give it to God. After all, we cannot all agree on everything or like everyone. That is simply how the world works and we have to get used to it. When we are able to understand that not everyone is going to like us, the need to have everyone like us dissipates, ridding us of one more burdensome stress or worry that many of us carry: namely, caring too much about what others think of us to the point of it causing stress and anxiety.

Obviously, as aforementioned, it is a different situation altogether when dealing with children or the elderly, for they need to be cared for and protected. Boundaries need to be navigated differently with these groups. Aside from these populations, when you maintain a healthy boundary and give up the need to change someone's mind by respecting their boundary, peace increases and life flows more smoothly, which likely increases happiness and contentment. It is normal to disagree. Accept it! Do not be bothered or care when disagreement with someone arises as, in reality, you will disagree with everyone if you talk long enough. Disagreement can lead to progress, healing, and a better situation in the end, at times.

Disagreement is natural. Be peaceful internally, regardless. Once again, as the axiom goes, we can never change someone else, their thinking or behavior, but we can change our reaction to them. In some cases, we can persuade another, but this is rare and we must be careful not to cross boundaries. It is rare because, often, opinions and beliefs operate at a deep level where emotions are attached, which outweigh logic for people in the end. Thus, modeling and living out what we think and believe is the best witness for others. St. Francis of Assisi is reported as saying something to the effect or sentiment: one should preach all the time, anywhere and everywhere, and use words only if necessary. How doing this on a grand scale could change the world. John Wesley echoed this sentiment later in history as well.

In terms of maintaining healthy boundaries while interacting with others in this world, it is good to view every encounter with someone as a divine encounter. See the divine or God in the other for we are all reflections of the image of God (Gen 1:27). As Mother Teresa said regarding daily encounters with people, try to ensure you leave them better than they were before. Show them grace in whatever way you can. Show them the face of God or Christ, but do this all while maintaining what is a healthy boundary for you, so you retain your peace and can then properly manifest *shalom* for yourself and them.

PRINCIPLE 6

Forgive

RELIGIOUS TRADITIONS HAVE LONG advocated the power of forgiveness. Before Yom Kippur, the Day of Atonement, Jews are called to forgive those who have wronged them and to ask for forgiveness from those they wronged. From a Christian perspective, it is often said in the pulpit: forgive as Christ forgave us. "And be kind to one another, tenderhearted, forgiving one another, as God in Christ has forgiven you." (Eph 4:32) Recall the Lord's Prayer: "Forgive us our trespasses as we forgive those who trespass against us."

Forgiveness is actually a commandment in the New Testament. We are only forgiven according to the measure we forgive: "For if you forgive others their trespasses, your heavenly Father will also forgive you; but if you do not forgive others, neither will your Father forgive your trespasses." (Matt 6:14–15). To some extent this is scary. Forgiveness can heal the soul as well as the body, and the decision is somehow in our own hands. The curative power of forgiveness was recently aired on the February 2nd, 2017 700 Club broadcast, a program of the Christian Broadcasting Network which has been controversial in the past. Irrespective of that, this broadcast told the story of a man named Al Matthias who had been diagnosed with multiple serious health issues and given only a couple of years to live. After trying everything, his sister told him she had been healed from ailments, specifically tumors in her breasts, a serious condition, by learning how to forgive others and suggested he give it a try. Though he thought her suggestion absurd, his desperation made him gave it a try. He began by forgiving his father for abandoning him and his family when he was a child. To his astonishment, he was completely healed of all his ailments and diseases. His doctors were at a loss to explain what had happened. He, concomitantly, renewed his faith in God and, more than fifteen years later now, has a counseling practice and ministry called Wellspring Ministries, which teaches people how to forgive. He claims to see thousands healed every year by simply teaching them how to forgive. This is a tangible example of how forgiveness actually heals. Jesus admonished people to forgive seventy times seven, which basically means all the time.

Empirical research confirms the beneficial effects of forgiveness. Not being at peace, or in a negative state, produces toxins that wreak havoc on the body and contributes greatly to unease and disease. A recent book, *Forgiveness and Health*, documents the wide-ranging health benefits of forgiving.[1]

Forgiveness is not for the person who needs to be forgiven, but for the one granting the forgiveness, for that person has a need to rid themselves of the negative emotions and thoughts surrounding a wrong that has been done to them. Such a person is still holding on to a past hurt and negative emotions of some sort, especially when that person directs their attention to another person or situation that brought pain. If you need to forgive someone, you have unfinished business which you need to resolve, so those negative emotions and thoughts do not arise when you think of the situation or person again later. When Jesus tells us to pray for those who persecute us (Matt 5:44), it is for ourselves as much as for our enemy that we should do it. We need to rid ourselves of the anger, bitterness, and unforgiveness in our heart. That the prescription Jesus gives is prayer reveals how prayer has a healing impact on a person, as it connects one to God. This is remarkable considering

1. Thoresen, Harris, and Luskin, *Forgiveness and Health*.

Jesus does not even elaborate here that we need to pray for forgiveness. Jesus knows that connecting to God via prayer will automatically bring that aspect when undertaken faithfully—more than just every now and then—among many other healing, transformative aspects.

Often when clients in therapy say they need to forgive someone, it means they really need to forgive themselves for perceived insufficiencies or shame, which can be either warranted or completely unwarranted. Forgiveness of self needs to occur. We need to rid ourselves of guilt and shame and, in the end, not be so hard on ourselves. We need to give ourselves grace, just as God gives us grace. We are way harder on ourselves than God is on us, so should we not try to emulate God and go easy on ourselves? We need to learn to value our self and love ourselves as God loves us. By way of our being human, we should love ourselves as God loves all of us, the entire human race. I once worked with a client who could not forgive, so I asked him to pray for the person he could not forgive, not in terms of praying the person sees where he wronged my client, praying for an apology, or praying that their relationship be mended. I asked him, simply, to pray for the other person's wellbeing, happiness and the like, so not in any self-serving manner. The client did and, after some time, a healing occurred. I recommend this to all and have seen its benefits for all involved. Such is commanded of us by Jesus, specifically, to pray for our enemies.

Do not let others have power over you. For your health, forgive. Let go of how others have hurt you and how you have disappointed yourself—that is, for what you perceive as wrong based on your particular belief system in regards to what you have done. Often you will find you do not even warrant carrying guilt and shame. Virtually always you do not, for we are forgiven. Recall we are all forgiven, so do not live like you are not. Embrace the forgiveness. It has been said that guilt is like a bag of rocks, just set it down. So, forgive yourself and others. Jesus was rather clear on this.

A lesson in forgiveness can be taken from those South Africans who fought the system of Apartheid in that country and who were, subsequently, unjustly put in prison for their efforts, oftentimes for decades. Nelson Mandela spent over twenty-seven years in prison. After their release from prison, many South Africans advocated forgiveness; Mandela being a prime example. In a few cases, the South Africans even became close friends with their Afrikaaner jailers, who themselves were descendants of the Dutch settlers who colonized the country decades before. If, after decades of being wrongly imprisoned, the human spirit can forgive such a crime, so can we forgive those who wrong us as Jesus commands.

There are other examples of people who suffered immensely at the hands of captors and then forgave. The story recently portrayed in the film *The Railway Man* of the English captive during WWII, played by Colin Firth, who was taken captive by the Japanese and was repeatedly beaten by a specific Japanese soldier is a case in point. He later suffered, no doubt, with what we now call PTSD. He then decided he was going to kill the soldier. On his way to do so, he had a transformative experience and encounter with him. He, eventually, forgave the soldier and the two became friends. This can serve as a model of forgiveness, for, if he can forgive, so can we. No matter how horrendous and egregious the damage done, with work, we can forgive anyone. Again, the forgiveness is first of all for the forgiver. In war cases as much as in child abuse, forgiveness brings new life.

Bob Marley said it best: "The truth is, everyone is going to hurt you. You just got to find the ones worth suffering for." Forgiving is rarely a one-time act. It is a process. Eventually, you will get to a point where you no longer need to work at forgiving anymore. There are multiple ways to do it. One is offered by the spiritual giant and peace activist, Thich Nhat Hanh, and his work on mindfulness and forgiveness. He implores people to forgive and suggests meditation for forgiveness. His classic, *Being Peace,* explains how forgiveness can occur by meditating compassionately on the suffering that a person you are engaged in conflict with went through, which helps understand why that person is acting in the way he or she does.[2] The number one ingredient in forgiveness is empathy.

This compassionate meditating is also meditating for insight, which is particularly helpful when you want to understand something or why someone has wronged you. You might also receive illumination that helps you realize the issues and problems other people are dealing with or, simply, that you can truly never understand what someone else has been through or is going through, and that whatever it is, it's likely rougher than you realize. In the latter case, sympathy for another might be engendered. The proverbial saying that you need be nice to everyone, for we are all fighting our own battles comes to mind. This practice of meditating for forgiveness engenders compassion and empathy even for enemies, and mitigates your anger toward them via understanding. Compassion and even love for the one who has wronged you ensues. Such a process could heal the world if we all did it. Merely contemplating the other helps. We also realize we can never truly know what someone else is going through; this is a big nugget of wisdom *Being Peace* provides. As we can never truly know what is going on with someone else, even a loved one or spouse, we should cut everyone some slack and forgive. As the Apostle Paul wrote to the church at Ephesus, "Be kind to one another, tenderhearted, forgiving one another, as God in Christ has forgiven you." (Eph 4:32) Do the same with yourself and peace will be manifested.[3]

Here is a simple meditation to start the forgiveness process:

MEDITATION FOR LOVE OR FORGIVENESS (10 MINUTES)

- Sit in a room and concentrate on your breathing.
- Still your mind.
- Then think of someone you love or something you love to do.

2. Hanh, *Being Peace*.
3. See also Wiesenthal, *Sunflower*.

- Once you have noticed what this positive feeling does through your whole body, and once you have allowed that positive feeling of love to impact your whole body and being, substitute the person you need to forgive in the place of the previous person or image.

- Allow the love and positive feelings to stay and radiate to the person substituted for as long as possible.

- Repeat the steps above as needed, or when the positive emotions dissipate and you need to bring back the positive emotions into your body and the positive image in your mind. Once the positive emotions and feelings are present again in the body, you can substitute the person needing forgiveness again.

Principle 7

Meditate and Connect to God

WE COME FROM GOD and to God we will return. We deceive ourselves when we think this life is about us and not God, for in God
we live and move and have our being (Acts 17:28). This is one of
the longer chapters of the book as it deals with a topic that is beyond full comprehension by our finite minds—the transcendent.

We are often anxious and fearful in our lives because we have
not taken the time to connect with God. God is always with us,
but we do not perceive God's presence. How can we connect to
God and, at times, even sense his abiding presence? The answer
is through prayer, meditation, and other means, such as through
sacraments and other rituals. We are certainly always connected
to God in our innermost being, but what follows allows us to live
into that reality better.

Many traditions maintain that our innermost being comes
from God and that we aspire to divinity. Mystics in most traditions
suggest that in the end we merge into God. The Cabbalists in Judaism and the Sufi mystics in Islam contend that the purpose of life
is to move along a trajectory that has its end in a union with God.
Meister Eckhart, Hui-Neng, St. Catherine of Sienna, and Thomas
Merton are but a few well-known examples arguing in this vein.

By cultivating meditation and prayer, even a minimal amount a day, our being will relax, remember we are connected to God, and thus be more at peace when daily stress arises. These practices allow us to tackle all that arises with an internal state of peace.

One common denominator between all spiritual giants, mystics, and saints is that they all set time aside daily to pray. The apostle Paul actually tells us to "pray without ceasing" (Luke 18:1; 1 Thess 5:17). If we want a relationship with someone, we must communicate with them. To have a relationship with God, we must communicate with him via prayer or meditation. Connect to God, however you do it or whichever way works best for you. Some people in the Catholic tradition connect through the mass and liturgy, through adoration, saying the rosary, centering prayer, meditation, mindfulness walking, or simply by walking in nature or going for a run. Whatever you do that works and allows you to connect to your source, make it a habit and do it, for it will recharge your batteries, so to speak, and connect you to your true source: God. It also staves off negative emotional states and ailments and brings inner peace, even in the midst of problems.

The major founders of the world religions practiced prayer and meditation, and their followers seek to emulate their respective founders. In the Abrahamic faith traditions, this can be seen with Hebrew Bible figures such as Moses, with Jesus, and with Muhammad in Islam. Recall the prophet Muhammad would go off to meditate on the outskirts of Mecca, in a cave called Hira. While meditating one day, he encountered the angel Gabriel and that meeting began the revelations which would later be recorded in the Qur'an. Prayer is an integral part of a spiritual life.

Several of the means by which we can connect to God, discussed below, are techniques therapists teach and have clients make use of, as they have been empirically studied and shown to be immensely helpful in relieving anxiety and other issues, particularly during stressful times. To a large extent, the counseling field has appropriated these practices, after having verified their efficacy in helping people. My clients have reported tremendous relief, whatever their particular faith tradition.

The psychology and counseling fields have co-opted techniques long used to connect to God, simply taking God out of the equation. With or without God, these techniques have proven therapeutic. A prime example is the use of mindfulness and meditation in therapy in cases of chronic pain, and how it has now branched off to help with other mental health issues. Despite initial resistance from the psychological and mental health profession, implementing spirituality into the therapeutic process can have enormous benefits.

It has been demonstrated that the level of a person's spirituality impacts mental health and well-being more so than a past trauma, such as abuse or a violent act, and in a positive manner.[1] This is reason enough to argue in favor of the inclusion of spirituality in counseling. Historically, mindfulness and meditation entered the counseling/psychology field because most practitioners were open to Eastern religious ideas and philosophies. Prayer and meditation (with or without reference to God) seek to connect us to the divine, where true healing and well-being originate, for in God we live and breathe and have our being (Acts 17:28). It is now time to look at a few ways to connect to God (Appendix B of this work contains additional practices).

PRAYER

It is said of St. Francis of Assisi that his unwavering discipline of prayer, along with virtuous living, gave him a "serenity of mind," that is, peace.[2] Taking the time to connect to God is a discipline. It is also akin to breathing. We must do it to enter into the spiritual life, beyond the illusion of the material world. I have never heard of anyone practicing prayer and meditation for an extended period of time and say it did not produce the sense of peace Jesus promised: "Peace I leave with you; my peace I give to you" (John 14:27).

1. Hipolito et al., "Trauma-Informed Care," 208.
2. See Bonaventure, quoted in Cook, *Francis of Assisi*, 74.

Prayer brings a true peace in the midst of ailment and problems, as well as the means and grace to learn how to manage a
tough situation. Though God can certainly heal anyone, a full
healing is not automatically granted this side of life. Learning how
to manage an illness or problem in peace during the process is
nevertheless possible, no matter the issue.

Prayer is our access to this peace or *shalom*. God does not
care how you do it, just do it. I know one person who uses a technique he also uses when he cannot sleep. He simply breathes in,
saying in his mind he is "breathing in the Holy Spirit" and, when
breathing out, mentally recites "out anxiety." This type of prayer
helps calm his anxiety as well as focuses him on the Holy Spirit. As
anxiety is so frequently accompanied by sleep disturbances, it is often the first thing to occur in the absence of peace. This, and other
techniques in this book, can also be helpful to engage in when you
are having a hard time sleeping.

THE JESUS PRAYER

The Jesus prayer is a favorite of mine; I highly recommend this
ancient and almost mystical practice. Granted, it presupposes a
Christian theology, but non-Christians can certainly try it or come
up with a similar prayer that coheres with their respective faith tradition and theology. Why not give it a try? There is nothing wrong
with experimenting, as someone experimented to come up with all
the techniques in this work and, undoubtedly, there are techniques
yet to be discovered.

The Jesus prayer goes all the way back to the desert fathers
in Egypt. Today, it is used by countless Orthodox monks and laity
alike who repeat it thousands of times a day. It was popularized in
more recent times by the anonymous Russian author who wrote
The Way of the Pilgrim, which was later made more well-known
in the West by J.D. Salinger's novel, *Franny and Zooey*. I have personally used the prayer in instances of distress and need, and it,
literally, calmed me down, and the situation I was dealing with
immediately resolved itself in a very positive way. This is but one

technique, for those of the Christian tradition, and can be made use of profitably by those outside of orthodoxy, such as Protestants.

Whatever your tradition, there are techniques unique to your specific faith that, no doubt, can be used profitably to help connect with God in a deeper way. For example, in Buddhism, some of its mantras are said to aid in a similar manner, an example being the Buddhist prayer, Nembustu, from Shin Buddhism. However, it should be noted that monks of the Orthodox faith are quick to point out that the Jesus prayer, technically, is not a mantra and, undoubtedly, a differing theology underlies this prayer from mantras of Eastern religions. Be that as it may, there are similarities and digging into your respective faith traditions and its history will reveal similar types of prayer you can make use of, likely ones that are repeated throughout the day and help reorient you to the spiritual world, or remind you that there is more than the material so that you can refocus and connect to God.

To engage in this simple prayer, repeat it over and over again, particularly in times of need. There are several versions. I recommend the ones with seven words or twelve words, both symbolic biblical numbers: "Lord Jesus Christ, have mercy on me," or "Lord Jesus Christ, Son of God, have mercy on me, a sinner."

Repetitions internalize the prayer. You eventually cease to say it on your lips, uttering it in your heart. It becomes second nature and a lived reality. This prayer can also be used when engaging in other forms of prayer and meditation, such as contemplative prayer or Christian centering prayer.

CHRISTIAN CENTERING PRAYER

To some extent, Christian centering prayer was introduced to the West by the work of Thomas Merton and his introduction of much Eastern thought. It can, however, be traced all the way back to the third century desert fathers in Egypt. This technique is highly effective. To some degree, it can be thought of as a helpful synthesis of Christian prayer and Eastern meditation practice. The foremost advocate of it today is, arguably, the priest Thomas Keating. His works on the topic include *Manifesting God* and *Intimacy with God: An Introduction to Centering Prayer*, among other works. A helpful video on the subject is *Thomas Keating: A Rising Tide of Silence*. He argues that the benefit of the practice comes during a person's waking life and not during the practice itself, which he says only needs to be done for twenty minutes a day. Obviously, doing it twice a day is optimal. The practice brings down anxiety and puts the practitioner into a calmer state both during and after the practice is over.

Here is the way Keating explains how to engage in the centering prayer:

- Choose a sacred word as the symbol for your intention to consent to God's presence and action within you.

- Sitting comfortably and with eyes closed, settle briefly, and silently introduce the sacred word as the symbol of your consent to God's presence and action within.

- When engaged with your thoughts, return ever-so-gently to the sacred word.

- At the end of the prayer period, remain in silence with eyes closed for a couple of minutes.[3]

It is, literally, that simple. I would add that you can actually use the Jesus prayer to do this practice or a favorite peaceful line of scripture, such as, "Be still and know I am God," or a peaceful image from Scripture. You can use such a phrase or image to begin the centering, or use it as a focal point and always return to the phrase/image when thoughts wander, as they will, which is completely normal and natural. I do not think you need be too rigid in how to engage in this practice. As my priest friend says, what a beautiful thing that you want to spend time with God and connect to God, no matter how you do it or how little time you spend doing it. Even five minutes a day is better than nothing. Again, whatever works best for you is argued here, as well as trying out different ways to find what is best for you, for one size does not fit

3. Keating, *Manifesting God*, 134–36.

all. After all, something is better than nothing, but I would ensure the phrase/image (if you choose to use one) is a loving and peaceful text, phrase, or image.

As was the case with Elijah who heard God in "a sound of sheer silence" (1 Kgs 19:12), Keating emphasizes that the language God speaks in is silence. Practice is often required to acquaint us and make us comfortable with silence. That is why it is helpful to try both ways to see what is best for you—using a sacred word or phrase as well as not using one, but teaching your mind to not think. Many spiritually inclined writers and mystics will agree that it is in silence we meet God, hear God and, ultimately, meet ourselves. The vehicle of silence provides the context for transformation and, thus, true, lasting peace that no one can take away or disrupt, no matter what.

It seems to be the case that we, all too often, spend much time in prayer engaged in one-way communication. We are always telling God what we need or want. Centering prayer affords us the opportunity to make it a true conversation, thus deepening our relationship with God by simply listening. God often talks to us during this time rather than when we ramble on to God about our needs, wants, and desires. I know a priest and psychotherapist who says he does an hour a day of centering prayer and always begins it by saying, "Here I am Jesus; your servant is listening." We truly need only sit in stillness and quiet and listen. Amazing insights can occur, but most often what happens occurs not during the prayer/meditation, but later in life, as Keating notes.

Data from a plethora of scientific studies reveals that meditation of this type has tremendous benefits, which include reduction in anxiety, stress, and a physiological increase in numerous aspects of health in the body and mind. Its impact on the spirit is certain as well. Numerous people have told me that they are, consequently, able to perceive things better and have much keener intuition, which they credit to their centering prayer time each day with God. And, of course, all tell me they are more at peace during their day. This is all because they have connected to their source, God, which is where we all came from and where we are all headed. Some people also find prayer during or after Scripture reading to be helpful and edifying. You can certainly add this if you find it helpful with centering prayer practice. Trying out different practices is recommended, though discipline is crucial. Whatever method is used, it must be given a fair amount of time to produce its fruits. Finding a spiritual director can also be helpful.

Centering prayer also reveals the interconnectedness of all humanity as Thomas Merton explains it in what has become known as his Louisville experience, on the corner of Fourth and Walnut, when looking around the shopping district:

> I was suddenly overwhelmed by the realization that I loved all those people, that they were mine and I theirs, that we could not be alien to one another even though we were total strangers. It was like waking from a dream of separateness . . . It was as if I suddenly saw the secret beauty of their hearts, the depths of their hearts where neither sin nor desire nor self-knowledge can reach, the core of their reality, the person each one is in God's eyes.[4]

Keating and others tell of similar stories to Merton's. The common thread in these experiences is that they occurred outside, when walking in mundane life, not during prayer time, but no doubt in large part because of their robust prayer life. The depth of a person's heart—the core of a person's reality—is where one encounters God in centering prayer. After the above quote, Merton writes that at the "center of our being" resides "a point of pure truth, a point or spark which belongs entirely to God." He goes on to say that this point "is the pure glory of God in us." And that, "It is, so to speak, His name written in us . . . like a pure diamond, blazing with the invisible light of heaven."[5] Perhaps this is the image of God (Gen 1:26) in us, or the Holy Spirit, the spark of the divine all humanity shares and what unites us all and, similarly, makes us all worthy of love and dignity.

4. Merton, *Conjectures*, 142, as cited in Pennington, *Thomas Merton*, 196–97.

5. Pennington, *Thomas Merton*, 197.

Merton was given access to the divine in all of us that connects us all because of his contemplative practice of connecting to God. Centering Prayer is how to connect to God. Centering prayer is, essentially, contemplative prayer which Merton's friend, the monk and scholar, Basil Pennington eloquently describes: "This freedom to let go of our rational control and open to the divine activity is developed in us through the practice of contemplative prayer." He goes on to say that it "provides the space for divine activity in our lives and calls it forth." It "spills over from our prayer time to all the other waking hours and even to the time of sleep."[6] Among other things, he is also intimating a manifestation of peace, for what spills over brings *shalom* to our lives.

The point Merton describes that resides at our very core is where we are still with God and reside in his love, a place that reorients us to the world and God, a place given to us by God and, perhaps, a part of God or God's spark in us. Many mystics say we are all sparks of the divine. Connecting to this spark connects us to our source. The cultivation of the connection to this center of our being and God is the key to peace, health, better intuition in life, and finding a meaning in life that is unsurpassed. It puts what matters in life into focus more readily, as well as our ultimate destiny. It wakes us up to God and is where our souls reside. In the process of attempting to go to our core, we also experience more peace, and the more time we spend in this place, or attempting to go there through meditation and prayer, the more we will manifest evergrowing amounts of peace which brings a multitude of healing, wholeness, and well-being.

CONDENSED VERSION OF ST. IGNATIUS' SPIRITUAL EXERCISES

The spiritual exercises of St. Ignatius of Loyola continue to help countless people through the ages, Jesuits and laity alike. The Jesuits or Society of Jesus was founded by Ignatius in the sixteenth

6. Pennington, *Thomas Merton*, 198–99.

century. The life of Ignatius, like that of Francis of Assisi, was one worthy of admiration in that during dire, crippling circumstances, both did not give up but rather used their pain and circumstances to reorient their lives to God and live for God. Ignatius' life is worthy of study for those seeking inspiration and insight, as are the lives of the saints in general. Saints, here, refers to the saints of the Christian church. There are numerous volumes and videos on the lives of the saints that have brought much inspiration and guidance to so very many. Many have been inspired and returned to their faith because of them, or simply been given faith after reading about them. I highly recommend studying the saints and reading about their lives. This alone could have been another chapter, as much wisdom, blessing, and peace arises out of learning about them.

The spiritual exercises of St. Ignatius grew out of his faith commitment. The exercises teach us to take time to meditate on the life and ministry of Christ, particularly the passion of Christ. Usually, it is done during retreats and comprises four parts, each of which contains extended daily prayer time and meditation on a portion of the life of Jesus. Here, again, the key is time with God in which God enlightens us because we become still, quiet, and listen and reflect on our essence and what God has done in history. Pope Francis used to prescribe this practice, and I know it was prescribed to him early in his life. This has been an immensely helpful spiritual exercise for people, not only those in the order, but also many in the laity. It is not widely known or made use of outside its respective faith community, although the practices are sometimes used by Protestants. These exercises, again, are Christian-oriented.

There is an amazing story about an academically-inclined man who struggled with aspects of his faith, especially the stories of the Bible, a common issue for academics and those acquainted with historical inquiry and modern scholarly methods of interpreting the Bible, such as source criticism. Apparently, the man undertook the spiritual exercises, and through prayer or contemplation of the passion, he specifically meditated on the cross, imagined himself there, and noticed what his senses perceived. During this type of meditation, while imagining touching the cross, this individual "was definitively relieved of his mental blockage,"[7] which somehow, mystically and supernaturally, allowed this person to transcend the issues with which he was struggling. This is the only such case I know of where an academic found resolution to this type of quandary so prevalent for religious scholars, especially biblical scholars. Are not all of us moderns plagued with similar types of questions/issues when it comes to our sacred texts and their stories, in our respective religious traditions, often on how to understand them today? Many of us moderns struggle with faith in the stories of our scriptures for, in having faith, they are more than just stories serving a didactic purpose or pithy wisdom sayings and tales. This man seems to have been given the faith and means to transcend this vantage point and step outside, or rather, above, such a limited perspective. He was given a new type or aspect of faith that deepened his view and opened his eyes. This reminds me of the words of Jesus when he explains, "then you will know the truth, and the truth will set you free" (John 8:32). Resolution to this man's issues was, perhaps, simply a by-product of the exercise—a helpful one. Who knows what other by-products Ignatian-type exercises could bring, along with helping to manifest peace in our lives? This story is a nice account of one way the spiritual exercises of Ignatius brought help and healing.

What is proposed here is a condensed version of what Ignatius suggested: taking time to meditate on the life of Christ and his passion or a text from the Gospels. The latter constitutes a practice that goes back into antiquity, all the way to Origen in the third century, and is known as Lectio Divina. Of late, it has become very popular among the laity, but it has always been an important practice among mystics, saints, and monastics in the Christian tradition. The monastic *Rule of Saint Benedict* calls for the practice and details how it should be done. Today, most advance a four-part process or movement to the exercise or actions of *Lectio Divina*: reading the Gospel text, meditating on it, praying on it, and contemplating it. The final stage entails a silence in which the

7. Tetlow, *Making Choices*, 73.

Holy Spirit is active in illuminating the text, among other things. Countless resources can be found online or in libraries to aid one in the process or discipline of *Lectio Divina*. You would be hard-pressed to find a mystic of the Western or Eastern Church who did not engage in the practice or allude to it in his or her writings. Think of Saint Augustine of Hippo, Thomas Aquinas, John of the Cross, Catherine of Sienna, Theresa of Avila or Therese of Lisieux (The Little Flower). The Second Vatican Council, as well as Pope Benedict XVI, have endorsed its use in recent years. Meditation on any of the Psalms is another tried and tested practice many today do profitably that, too, has its origins in the practices of the saints of the church. If Christianity is not your faith tradition, meditate on the central figure of your tradition, if there is one. Meditate on the lives and teachings of Buddha, Muhammad, or any other spiritual figure. As with all the other techniques outlined in this work, see if it is a fit for you and if results ensue after an extended period of time of practice. If it does not work for you, discard it. What works for one person will not necessarily be of help to another. Experimentation is important.

MEDITATION AND MINDFULNESS

The practice of meditation or simply mindfulness can be done either from a perspective of belief in God or without any such belief. Regardless of which, both can be highly effective in wellness, healing and peace. You can meditate without connecting to God and it is well-known that this alone has very positive effects, though, in that case, I might argue you would be connecting to God without realizing it. Short meditations, such as five-minute meditations, exist on the internet and in numerous literary sources. Appendix B at the end of this book provides some such techniques the present author recommends.

The practice of meditation can be done to bring about change and peace in your life. This practice simply involves being still, either by sitting in a lotus position or in a chair, and not thinking. You can concentrate on your breathing, or anything else, and let that be the sole focus. When your mind wanders, you can bring it back to your breath or to what is described as "nothing" or "not thinking." When a thought comes, you are then to release it, or let it come to mind, then let go. Everyone will have "monkey mind" at first but, with practice, you learn to focus on the "nothing" and, consequently, feel a sense of peace, which increases with practice. It helps to function in the day, relieving much stress and anxiety. The data on the effects of doing this daily are nothing short of amazing. Its efficacy has been proven time and time again with regard to its impact on mental and physical well-being. If this practice is too hard at first, you can use videos from the internet. Wayne Dyer and Deepak Chopra have some excellent ones online.

Many report the "nothingness" state you can reach in this practice, at times, to be an illuminating, mystical experience of sorts. This is intriguing, though it is not the norm. Perhaps God gives us what we need and some do not need it. A particularly interesting holy man from India, Shivapuri Baba, is reported to have lived to a very old age. He said the following: "First, what we have got to do is: discipline this life, then meditate on God. When you see God, every problem is solved."[8] Paramahansa Yogananda, who wrote *Autobiography of a Yogi* and introduced Kriya Yoga to the West, made similar points.[9]

GUIDED IMAGERY:
CREATING PATHWAYS IN THE BRAIN

For healing, better functioning and success in life, many make use of guided imagery. Many professional athletes use this technique and report greatly enhanced performances. It involves imagining what you want to occur in your body or life repeatedly in your mind. This often entails a healing in part of your body or success in some activity. During a quiet sitting session, you envision or imagine, repeatedly, what you desire: hitting a home run in a

8. Bennett, *Long Pilgrimage*, 46.

9. Yogananda, *Autobiography*.

baseball game, remaining calm during a big speech, or healing part of the body of an ailment such as cancer. It, literally, creates new connections and pathways in your brain. When you engage in the activity of imagining, the pathways are already present to help best facilitate the activity. That the brain has a role in the healing of the body is without doubt. It facilitates healing in the body when it is needed. Guided imagery not only helps create healing pathways in the brain, but strengthens them each time one engages in the practice.

Tony Robbins recently did an experiment on a nationally televised morning news show while promoting a new book of his. He had people twist their torso as far as they could go. Afterward, he had the group imagining doing it again twice, but going further in their mind only. Then the people repeated the exercise about a minute later and they were able to twist their torso much further. He correctly noted that their belief changed in some way with the guided imagery and this changed what they could do. It shows the power of belief. It is also the case that imagining what they could do created new pathways and connections for the change before it ever occurred, helping to facilitate it when it did occur in real time.

Advances in neurocognitive sciences show that during guided imagery new pathways are created in the brain. People, simply by thinking about something, often create new pathways. Thinking about something repeatedly, makes it permeant. Negative thinking becomes permanent when you dwell on the negative. The good news is that the brain can create new pathways and, with some effort, old maladaptive pathways can be destroyed. By applying some of the principles in this book, room for new, adaptive neural pathways can supplant the old ones. This is a very important point. Numerous books have been written on the subject and this will prove to be an important field in the future.[10]

10. On neuroplasticity, see Leaf, *Switch on Your Brain*, and Dispenza, *You Are the Placebo*.

These are but a few of the practices that can allow you to better connect with God, our true source. If you want a relationship with someone, you must communicate with that person. So, if you want a relationship with God, then you must talk to God. How do you do that? Through prayer and the other teachings discussed here. You cannot be close to God, or, at least, feel God's presence and make use of God's guidance without setting time aside daily to commune with him. That often will be when we truly learn about ourselves, the real impediments to our peace, how to rectify issues we might not realize we are dealing with, and find solutions for our problems, all the while in the context of communing with our maker, where peace becomes more manifest in our lives.

Connecting to God via prayer and meditation also connects us with humanity as a whole. An experiment involved two individuals meditating in a room beside one another while hooked up to a machine that screened their respective brains. When one eye was pried open and a light shined into it a section of that person's brain lit up. What is astounding is that the other person's brain lit up at the exact same time in the exact same regions though her eyes remained shut. The experiment was done again with the person in another room with the same results. Only one flashlight was shined in one eye and it affected the other person in the same manner when they were both engaged in the activity of connecting to God. They were connected to God and, thus, in some mystical way, better connected to each other, tangibly displaying humanity's and God's inter-connectedness. This is all documented in the wonderful documentary entitled *I Am*.

We are connected in ways we do not even realize, as Buddhist traditions have long articulated. The same movie, *I am*, shows that there is a heartbeat within a heartbeat that suggests a person's emotional state. Again, when two people meet, the heartbeats pick up on the other's beat. On an unconscious level, our being knows the state of another without needing to convey it in words. The two heartbeats will often mimic each other. This is, perhaps, what is meant when we say I liked or did not like that other person's energy. It is, literally, energy humans pick up on with each other. We should also recall animals are excellent at picking up on humans' energy, as are little children, a topic wholly worthy of another manuscript. This discussion is all very consistent with the Buddhist emphasis on the interconnectedness of all sentient beings. What a profound truth this is.

A Russian study has demonstrated that a cell in the mouth of a person in pain produces a typical reaction. When a human subject in the experiment was pricked with something, the cell reacted. The study revealed that, even after the cell was taken out of the person's body and removed two blocks away in the city, when the person was pricked, the cell still reacted despite the distance from the person's body at the exact time the person was pricked, as though it was still connected to the person. This goes to show how little we know about how the universe works. It is beyond the finite capacity of our minds.

For this reason, there is a tension among religious people and traditions on the issue of God's transcendence versus God's immanence. Yet, many religious people would agree that "All religions exist for the sole purpose of assisting believers to conquer their humanness and its litany of frailties and then achieve a god-like identity, with all its glory."[11]

The great rabbi Hillel (110 BCE–10 CE) was once challenged by a gentile who promised to convert to Judaism if Hillel taught him the whole Torah while standing on one foot. Hillel converted him, saying: "That which is despicable to you, do not do to your fellow. This is the whole Torah, and the rest is commentary, go and learn it" (Babylonian Talmud, *Shabbat* 31a).

As we are all connected, so must we do unto others as we want for ourselves. Remembering the Golden Rule and putting it into practice is vital. What we do to others, we do to ourselves. Practicing the methods outlined in this book help us connect to God and increase our ability to better discern what we should do in a situation, adopting a discernment that aligns us with God's

11. Chitakure, *Pursuit of Sacred*, 92.

desire, fosters health, wholeness, true happiness and, importantly, peace. Said differently, this practice of connecting to God, however you do it, better enables you to listen to your intuition, which will tell you what is best for you in any given situation. Some call it intuition, others the Spirit or Holy Spirit, which dwells inside of us and wants what is best for us, pointing us in the direction of peace, if we listen. Your intuition will often warn you of danger. If your intuition makes you feel that you are not at peace about something, listen to that. These meditations and prayers will help you better cultivate the ability to listen to your intuition.

PRINCIPLE 8

Watch and Alter
Thoughts as Needed

OUR THOUGHTS HAVE A monumental impact not only on our mental and physical well-being, but on the trajectory and outcome of our lives. Echoing earlier Greek philosophers, the Roman Emperor Marcus Aurelius, stated in the second century CE, "Our life is what our thoughts make it." With the advent of process theology and quantum physics, it is being scientifically demonstrated how our thoughts actually manifest our reality or, said differently, we manifest and cause what we think. Our thoughts truly create our reality.

The case can be proven by a very simple experiment. Simply sit down and think about a situation that made you nervous in the past then think about a situation that made you feel relaxed and calm. You will notice that, in thinking about those times, you will experience the same or a slightly subdued amount of the same emotions. You will notice, almost immediately, your entire body responds, especially your heart rate. The nervous situation you recall will actually increase your heart rate, which affects your entire body, and the calming situation will then bring a reduced pulse and calm to your entire being. This is all done just by your thoughts.

The implications of this knowledge are profound. Just as we can create our realities and positive states of well-being and peace, so, too, we can create and perpetuate negative states. Unfortunately, all too often, we get stuck in thoughts that not only serve us poorly, but contribute greatly to malady, mental disease, and overall disruption in our lives. For whatever reason, research is showing humans beings have a natural tendency to think of themselves negatively by default. It seems to be innate and ingrained. This tendency needs to be addressed by anyone who seeks a life of peace. The solution is to watch and alter thoughts, as needed.

Negative thoughts and core beliefs are often conditioned by things that happened in our childhood. Victims of abuse often have a core belief that they are unworthy and unlovable and have done something wrong. If not addressed, an abuse victim can carry these beliefs, thoughts, and feelings for their entire life, which can have an impact on every domain of life. Self-esteem and confidence are usually greatly diminished. The good news is that these core beliefs and thoughts can be changed, which then allows for healing, better emotional functioning, and peace. This chapter will show you how to change negative core beliefs.

It is possible that all behaviors arise out of either fear or love and, it can be argued, emotions can all be distilled down to either positive or negative ones. Our specific cultures name and define the nuanced positive and negative emotions we all have.

Negative emotions are not beneficial and the ultimate, supreme positive emotion is love. As every mystic or saint in every religious tradition explains, we ultimately merge back into God into a state of union with God; "God is love" (1 John 4:8b). Love is thus what we should strive for, constantly striving to operate out of a positive emotional state and doing what we can to get out of negative emotional states. When we operate out of love, we have true peace as we are in closer proximity to God and this radiates throughout our entire being to others. This state of loving peace also brings with it a higher degree of intuition, which makes sense as we are more connected to God.

By contrast, anger, for instance toward Muslims, is unfortunately common today. I see this as acting out of fear, a negative emotional state that, no doubt, serves a purpose in some instances. It is in a negative state of being that we forget we are all God's children. If we catch this and realize we are not acting out of love in such instances and change our thoughts and corresponding negative emotions, we will be more at peace and, if done on a grand scale, the world would be too. Peace is manifested by adapting our thoughts to a more realistic and accurate evaluation of our actual situation.

To do this, we must watch and alter our thoughts as needed. This posture applies to our perceptions of others, as well as to how we view ourselves. Bob Marley astutely said, "Emancipate yourselves from mental slavery; none but ourselves can free our minds." Watching and catching your thoughts and altering them to more adaptive, realistic ones as needed, especially when you find yourself in a negative place, is how you emancipate your mind. It has helped millions to transform their lives, even veterans and others struggling with PTSD, severe trauma, depression, and a host of other conditions.

Catching your thoughts and changing them from maladaptive, inaccurate, and negative ones to more adaptive, realistic, and positive ones is cognitive behavioral therapy (CBT) and is associated with the psychiatrist, Aaron Beck. In the sixties, Beck discovered that virtually all of his depressed patients shared negative maladaptive thinking. What is more, he discovered most of his clients thoughts on this score were wrong or inaccurate. He began to work with his patients to change their thoughts and deeper beliefs. He observed that, when they did, the vast majority of them got better. It had long been known that what a person thinks has an effect on their person and life, but Beck combined elements of cognitive therapy and behavioral therapies into a framework that many mental health care providers use today to treat a host of mental issues with much success.

Beck realized that his patients' thoughts kept them depressed. Basically, it is really not about what happens to us, but rather how we perceive what happens that has the most impact on our mental and physical health. Our perceptions of events are, more often than not, more important than the actual event itself. For this reason, we are often our own worst enemy and our perceptions of events and thoughts can keep us in a hostile environment. Principle 8 provides a means to become our own best friend and liberate ourselves.

No doubt, we are influenced by what we spend time thinking about. We are influenced by what we read and watch; those things, literally, change our thoughts, so it is imperative to spend time thinking about the positive, not the negative, on what is edifying. Thinking new thoughts repeatedly creates new neuropathways and previous ones can be decommissioned or undone, which is good news for our negative thoughts in that they can be eliminated. We deceive ourselves if we think that what we think about does not have a profound impact on our entire being and life. Even watching a movie that is dark or negative in nature will have a bearing on our emotional state immediately, during and after for some time, as does spending time with negative people or other negative influences. As the saying goes, but with people in mind, if you lay down with dogs, you will get up with fleas. We need to watch how we spend our time and what we think and focus on. Christian theology holds that the body is the temple of the Holy Spirit, where God comes in and resides, so we must be careful what we allow in via our eyes and what then penetrates our thoughts.

We manifest what we think, to some degree. When we read certain books or listen to certain people or ideologies, we gradually internalize their positions and leanings, or are at least influenced by them, so it is important to "Set your minds on things that are above, not on things that are on earth" (Col 3:2).

It is now time to examine the solutions or techniques we can use when we realize we are having negative thoughts, holding negative beliefs, or experiencing negative emotional states. The solutions provide tangible ways of enabling relief and facilitating better thoughts, beliefs, and positive emotional states.

COGNITIVE BEHAVIORAL
THERAPY APPROACH

As what happens to us matters less than how we react to life events, how can we internalize this truth and practically alter our negative thoughts, which cause so many issues? How can we heal from the negative thoughts and the mental ailments they produce or exacerbate? It is easier than you think. According to CBT, we need to identify when a negative emotion arises and to observe what we are thinking. Then, the work is to ascertain what the deeper belief behind the thought is. It may be "I am a failure," or "I am worthless." More often than not, this thought or belief is not entirely accurate. Often, by realizing this alone, there is relief and healing, but more so when we replace the thoughts and beliefs with more realistic and accurate thoughts.

Here is an example: someone's side might hurt and they will then have the thought "I might have cancer." This causes tremendous fear and worry. Jumping directly to the worst-case scenario and thinking, what is, statistically, the more improbable reason for the pain, thinking the worst and the negative, inaccurate thought causes havoc for a long time. By altering the thought to a more realistic one, peace ensues. A more realistic thought is: there are numerous reasons my side could be causing pain, such as gas, and if it does not get better, I will go to the doctor, but I am not going to worry about it now because I cannot do anything about it at present. I will see if I even need to go to the doctor about it later. By retelling ourselves this when the thought that it might be cancer comes to mind, calming can occur. Some even choose to carry a card in their pocket and to take it out and read this alternative thought when negative emotions, such as anxiety, arise because of the negative, maladaptive, and inaccurate thoughts.

A thoughts record can also be helpful in this process, especially in determining the negative thoughts and seeing their relationship to negative emotions. It is also recommended to make use of a therapist who uses CBT to engage in this process. To identify the thoughts, find patterns in them when they arise, and figure out more accurate thoughts by disputing them, a thought record can be downloaded from the internet or you can create one using the following rubric:

- Event

- Location & time

- Negative emotion

- Automatic thought or belief

- Evidence for thought

- Evidence against thought

- Alternative, more accurate thought

- Feeling after repeating new thought several times

Disputing the irrational belief, so you can really see how it is not completely logical or accurate, is key in this process. A therapist spends a lot of time doing this when they engage with a client in CBT. It is often done in a Socratic questioning type of way. The self-directive CBT approach advocated here can be used for virtually any issue as, at the end of the day, it is all cognitive. Our thoughts impact and direct everything we do. The core of so many issues arises with our thoughts or is perpetuated by them. So, you can catch and alter your thoughts for relief when experiencing anxiety, depression, or any negative emotion. This approach can also be used for such things as overeating, self-confidence issues, and even relationship problems. It can even help with spiritual issues, such as someone struggling with one of the seven deadly sins. Gluttony, for example, can be attacked via addressing thoughts using the CBT approach.

DISTRACTION APPROACH

It is immensely important to catch your thought and stop ruminating on it. When you find yourself caught in this downward cycle, distract yourself by doing something else immediately. Go for a walk and partake in the cathartic and healing effect of just being in nature (as the data demonstrates), call a friend, say a rosary, however you self-sooth; just do not sit there and continue to dwell on the negative. An approach that comes out of dialectical behavioral therapy (DBT), which really grows out of CBT and incorporates mindfulness and other ideas, is to grab a piece of ice and hold it in your hand to distract yourself. This is helpful for people and has proved effective for those wanting to distract themselves when thoughts and emotions associated with eating disorders arise. This can be used when you need to distance yourself from anything negative.

To be fair, you can argue that mindfulness, which will be addressed below, really is a form of distraction when used to address anxiety and other issues, though it is more than just a distraction. Mindfulness breathing, feeling, walking, and other things can all be used to help distract yourself from ruminating thoughts, fearful thoughts, and obsessive, intrusive thoughts—such as fixating on a conversation, issue, or fear. Recently, I told a client to use this technique when she started to ruminate on a conversation she had with a person she does not get along with. She would go over the conversation without end in her mind, which never helped. In fact, it led to negative problems and depression. So, holding a piece of ice for a few seconds in her hand was designed to help her distance herself from her thoughts and then to stop her from ruminating on the conversation. The ice allows her to associate something negative with a particular thought in the hope of reducing the recurrence of the thought (operant conditioning). At the least, the use of ice will produce a long enough delay to help her figure out what she can do, and focus away from ruminating on the negative to engage instead in what will be helpful.

Spending time in nature by going for a walk is a good medicine, as exercise is an antidepressant. If you cannot walk, simply sitting outside in nature and taking a few deep breaths is very helpful. Just imagine how much more helpful this could be if you live by the sea or a body of water and are able to spend time by it. How much these simple techniques can help and heal should not be underestimated. Other techniques, including coloring a mandala, drawing, or doing a puzzle—whatever helps you self-sooth can be useful in helping you move from a negative to a positive emotional state. Thus, distracting yourself by whatever healthy means, even by something that you do not like, is important. You need to be on the lookout to catch the negative thought or behavior that is causing a lack of peace and stop it. Then it is helpful to do something that moves you to a positive emotional state via self-soothing.

SCHEDULE TIME TO WORRY
& SCRIPTURE THOUGHT REPLACEMENTS

Another technique is to set aside time each day or schedule a set time in the day you allow yourself to worry about whatever is bothering you (no longer than thirty minutes), and not let yourself worry about it otherwise. Catch and stop the thought during the day and do not let yourself worry about it, except during the allotted time you allow yourself to worry each day. When you catch the thoughts that bring worry or feel yourself going into a negative emotion, say to yourself, no, I am not going to allow myself to worry about this now, but I will worry about this later during my allotted time. Simply say "not now" and you can write down your worry, if you so desire, to look at it during your allotted time. You can also then practice the technique of distraction, outlined above, when you need a break from a negative, fearful thought or its corresponding negative emotions. Simply do something else, such as take a walk. Along with distraction, it will likely be helpful if you also have yourself recite a scriptural verse in your mind at this point such as, "I will never leave you or forsake you" (Heb 13:5), or, "Be still and know that I am God" (Ps 46:10). Whatever speaks to you and brings peace or makes you orient yourself to God is appropriate on this score. A wonderful resource for appropriate texts can be found in the free booklet you can find online, entitled "Thought Conditioners," by Norman Vincent Peale.[1] He details forty helpful scriptural verses with brief, insightful notes on each verse. A physician friend provides this book to all his patients. This book, the practice of setting aside a time to worry, along with distraction techniques, and calling to mind scriptural texts have all proven effective for many of my counseling clients.

MINDFULNESS APPROACH

This approach is helpful for those who do not have enough success with altering their thoughts. While the CBT approach tackles troublesome and detrimental thoughts head-on, this approach is more passive in its application with regard to the intrusive thoughts causing the issues. This technique does not avoid the thoughts, as avoidance does not address the problem and can make matters worse, but rather confronts the thoughts, or one could say accepts and even embraces them. This technique is in line with the counseling theory known as acceptance and commitment therapy (ACT). Now, if addressing thoughts and trying to alter them proves ineffective, there is another highly effective technique, which comes from Eastern religious traditions, particularly Buddhism. It is mindfulness. Instead of changing the negative, unwanted intrusion of a thought, simply observe it. Befriend it, perhaps, and it might lose its potency. Say to it, "Oh, hi there, it is you again." Very important: do not judge the thought or yourself for having it. Just say "hi" to it like a person in the street. You are not the thought. It just arose. Non-judgment is key. Realize it is present and how the thought affects your entire body, mind, and spirit. And then go on your way. No need to ruminate on it. Just welcome it. It works! Rumi's famous poem, *The Guest House*,

1. Peale, "Thought Conditioners. For a free downloadable copy of his thought conditioners, see: https://gaurang.org/pub/thought-conditioners-norman-vincent-peale.pdf."

enjoins us to welcome problems and challenges as much as joys, and to entertain them all as unexpected visitors, "even if they are a crowd of sorrows, who violently sweep your house empty of its furniture," because in fact these sorrows may be "clearing you out for some new delights."[2]

What seems horrendous is to be embraced, for it comes to teach us and help us grow in some way (see Principle 12). This coheres with Paul's words, "We know that all things work together for good for those who love God, who are called according to his purpose" (Rom 8:28).

There are several types of thoughts to be on the lookout for, particularly when you start to feel negative emotions. These thoughts can serve as warning signs, which let you know when something is off.

Perfectionist and Rigid Thinking

Perfectionist thinking and rigid thinking, such as all-or-nothing thinking, are often subtle, below the surface ideas and they often present together. We often, mistakenly, think we have to be right all the time or be perfect, especially when we think we have to be right to earn someone's approval or love. Such views often drive our behavior and cause us much grief; when we are not perfect, which is often, we then view ourselves as failures and negative emotions will arise. We must recall, we are all worthy as children of God created in God's image. Albert Ellis has shown that telltale signs of rigid thinking and perfectionist thinking are present when someone has a lot of self-talk, which is often actually expressed in phrases such as "I should have," "I must," or "I have to." These suggest rigid thinking and need to be addressed, or else the risk of being too harsh on ourselves and others can occur, with a concomitant increase in negative emotions, such as anxiety and depression and, thus, a disruption of peace.

2. Barks, *Essential Rumi,* 109.

"I should," "I must," or "I have to" are extreme ways of thinking that allow no leeway. Flexibility is thus, in part, the antidote. These rigid ways of thinking make us feel trapped. Often rigid thinking such as, "I must make an A on this exam," arises out of feelings of worthlessness or incompetence. This thinking is part of overcompensation or a misplaced assumption that our worth or someone else's love for us is contingent on how well we do. Again, in reality, you are worthy because you are a child of God. Therefore, every human being is worthy and has an innate dignity that does not derive from the usefulness of a person.

The thought-record rubric provided above can help identify the faulty thinking, so you can start to correct it and have better emotional health and well-being by trying to be realistic while continuing to watch out for perfectionist thinking. Here is a way to counter it:

- Tell yourself there is no such thing as perfection in this life.
- Do not be too hard on yourself, and remember unrealistic expectations sets you up for failure.

I have personally experienced how letting go of the need to always be perfect can be so freeing in life, for we can never be perfect all the time. You can always strive to do your best and that is fine, but things will sometimes go wrong or it might not be enough and that is OK. Sometimes your best is not enough and that is OK. Often things are out of your control and someone else messes up and that, in turn, makes you look bad or affects your efforts. However, when you let go of the need to be perfect or to be perceived that way, especially in work contexts, it is very freeing and worry/anxiety truly dissipates, for an unhelpful need or desire has been removed. Buddhist traditions can be helpful on this score, as they maintain that our problems arise out of our desires. If we control or temper them, things go better. All you can do is your best and not worry about the rest. The rest is up to God. Catching your thoughts and beliefs, with regard to perfectionist thinking, is vital. Real growth arises after learning to catch these thoughts and altering them. Oftentimes, unwittingly, parents impart negative thoughts on a child and they internalize them, thus conditioning them into negative, perfectionist, and rigid thinking. A dear friend recently told me that one of his parents would never say "Good job!" for getting a 97 on a test, but rather "Why did you miss one?" This led to perfectionist thinking that was only overcome later in life. In childhood, the thinking led to depression and even suicidal thoughts. Like so many other problems, it can become a vicious cycle, if not broken. If you are a perfectionist, you can pass this on to your children who, in turn, pass this type of thinking on to their children. This is not to blame parents, but to make them aware. Be the one to break the cycle, as freedom comes when you do. Remember: don't be so hard on yourself. We all mess up and fall short (Rom 3:23). Be kind to yourself. You are probably kinder to others. In reality, you need to be kind to others and yourself.

Self-sabotaging

We humans often sabotage our own peace. There is an irony or paradox of human nature, which I am not sure we really fully understand, though it can be overcome via the insights from religion and psychology outlined in this book. Namely, human behavior is often such that we do the exact opposite of what we want, or we do the exact opposite of what would allow for or bring us what we desire. For example, we want our spouses to be closer to us so, often unconsciously, we pick a fight with them, as it gives us some level of closer interaction, But, in the long run, it drives them the other away. We want closeness, yet we pick a fight. Or we want someone to love us, yet we act in ways that promote the opposite. Similarly, we tend to choose romantic partners that mimic the parent who hurt us the most in childhood because we have unfinished business inside of us. Sometimes people who have been abused continuously pick abusers as romantic partners or grow up to be abusers.

This phenomenon describes what is called self-sabotaging. We all do it to some extent because it served as a protective method or defense mechanism in childhood—which likely served us well then, but no longer does once we grow into adults. The good news is that we can break the cycle and learn to work on and improve our innate human inclination and the learned disposition toward self-sabotage. Change is always possible and it is never too late.

We need to know ourselves and the specific issues we have first before we can work on them and, eventually, change. We can become better versions of ourselves by overcoming the issues we have from childhood that lead us to self-sabotage, and it does not mean our caretakers were wrong or evil. It is hard to raise kids and often people get it wrong. Have grace with them on this score. We need to learn our issues first; we all have blind spots. Catch yourself when you find you are self-sabotaging, address the corresponding thoughts, and deal with them wisely. Finding a good therapist and truly engaging in the therapeutic process can be helpful in learning about yourself, your blind spots, and what you need to do to change and stop self-sabotaging.

Catastrophizing

This is rather common. It is when we imagine the worst case scenario, as demonstrated in the anecdotal story above regarding someone automatically thinking the pain in their side is cancer as opposed to a more likely cause of the pain. Another common example is when we hear a siren and actually think or assume it might be headed to a loved one's house. Catastrophizing is simply when we assume the worst is going to happen. Some say when we assume it is going to go bad, the worst is more likely to happen, a kind of manifest destiny.

We need to catch this in its tracks. This maladaptive way of thinking is the bringer of much anxiety. Catching thoughts and making them more realistic reduces much anxiety and forms a habit of thinking more realistically and helpfully. Sometimes, even only catching the thought and realizing it is not realistic has much benefit, as noted already, in reducing the negative consequences of the thinking.

Thus, we need to watch our thoughts, especially in terms of thinking the worst-case scenario, for, ironically, this is often the least likely outcome. When we think in such terms and begin to feel negative, emotions arise, such as anxiety or depression. These can be dealt with and overcome by changing our thoughts, even adapting them minimally. The data from psychology, specifically CBT and its insights, are very clear on this score.

Going Negative

It is important to be on the lookout for when you just generally go negative with your thoughts, as they will often lead to either depression or anxiety. Often, just noticing when you are upset all of a sudden will show you that there is virtually always a corresponding thought or belief that gave rise to the feeling or emotion. Figure out what the negative thought is; sometimes this takes some time and introspection. Catch and rework the negative thought(s) or image with more realistic adaptive thoughts. Catch your thoughts when you notice you are focusing on the negatives in something, your situation, a person and the like, or your day will be spent in the negative and this has implications for your peace and health. I do this. For example, when I begin thinking about a co-worker who has done me wrong, I notice I am going negative and immediately catch that thought and say, "Not going to go there." I choose to distract myself, think about something else, and not go negative. You can also choose to think about that person's good qualities or the good they have done for you, if you can. Refocusing is helpful in not going negative.

When you perceive the negative thoughts, and some are subtler or further beneath the surface than others, say to yourself, "I am going negative. What can I do to go positive?" Then shift to something positive, such as, "Thank God for giving me another day." You can call it the power of positive thinking. And it works. It also needs to be said that you should not beat yourself up for having the negative thoughts in the first place. This is normal and part of the human condition. There is no way to eradicate them, so do not try and set yourself up for failure. We have to struggle against it constantly in this life, but with practice it becomes easy to pivot into positive thoughts and beliefs that give way to positive emotions and a positive mental, as well as physical, state, thus making it easier and easier to manifest peace.

In addition to watching out for the pitfalls in cognition noted above, and altering the associated thoughts as needed, other noteworthy postures and techniques with regard to how we think are immediately helpful.

PERSPECTIVE IS KEY

"But strive first for the kingdom of God and his righteousness, and all these things will be given to you as well. So do not worry about tomorrow" (Matt 6:33–34). These words of Jesus point to where our thoughts should spend their time and thus where our perspective is best directed. Interestingly, Jesus tells us not to worry about the future, which is known to predispose us toward anxiety. Mystics and saints of every religious tradition echo this and often demonstrate it in their lives. Jesus' words provide the foundation here for how our perspective, thoughts, and lives should be oriented. That is the bottom line. Notice the very next words in this text of Jesus, after he implores us to strive first for God and his kingdom: we are not to worry. This implies that peace comes from having this perspective and actively striving first for God. We do that by what we focus on with our thoughts.

Jesus often answers a question with a question, and elsewhere asks, "And can any of you by worrying add a single hour to your span of life?" (Luke 12:25) Instead of constantly ruminating on your problems, look up. Refocus and your issue will be placed in its proper perspective.

Perspective is key. Additionally, adopting a thankful perspective, in spite of everything that is going on around you, pays dividends for your mental state and happiness. By cultivating an attitude of gratitude that thanks God for being able to breathe one more breath, live one more day, and see someone you love or a beautiful sunset, your peace increases dramatically. Perspective is key and cannot be overestimated. Think of life as a gift not a right and your perspective changes to gratitude and thankfulness. Realizing that it is not always going to go your way, but that is OK, is also an important posture. It contributes in no small measure to a proper attitude, happiness, and peace.

CONSTANTLY REFRAME

Reframe your situation constantly, especially when you are in a negative state or seeing something negatively—for example, instead of carrying on an internal dialogue that says, "I have to do this," reframe it and say, "I get to do this." This is an example of reframing. Instead of thinking/saying, "This stinks," say internally, "This is where I am standing and I will learn from this." You reframe the negative into the positive, which is always possible. There is often a silver lining or reason for the maddening suffering. I observed my former supervisor make use of this technique often in her work with much success.

An example of reframing is as follows: instead of saying to yourself, "This is bad and hurts," say, "This is a moment to learn and grow." Thus, it is all about attitude. If you have a major problem and do not care for someone, such as a co-worker, but must deal with them, instead of dwelling on the fact that you have a problem with them, you can ask yourself, "What can I learn from this situation?" or "How can I become a better person by having to deal with this?" This technique also does not allow for ruminating on the problem, which makes things worse. It is saying to yourself: "How can I learn to rise above and transcend this problem?" This will prove a skill you can use in other situations.

CULTIVATE AN ATTITUDE OF GRATITUDE

As noted above, cultivating an attitude of gratitude is another technique that helps greatly in the pursuit of manifesting peace in our lives. Life is a gift. Our hearts only beat another beat by the will of God and if God so desires. So enjoy every moment of life. Take time to laugh and have fun; don't take yourself too seriously all the time. Pain will come and go and we should all try to enjoy life in spite of the presence of pain, struggle, and hardship. These are a part of life. They cannot be avoided, but should be embraced for the gifts and growth they often, eventually, bring forth. Be thankful for it all: the good and the bad. After all, we only live and breathe another breath by the grace and providence of God. This goes along with perspective. This view will bring much peace, contentment, and happiness. Try this approach to see if it works for you. It does take practice, but the more practice, the better one will get. This one technique also has the power to change your life and give you a profound level of peace in your life. It also has the power to make you realize it is not all about you. It makes you realize it all works out in the end so there is no reason to fear, which you can only see after some time of living in this perspective.

Start looking at life as a gift, adopt a gratitude perspective and be thankful for all the little things. When you view life as a gift, it changes everything. It changes your perspective, from a view of drudgery and "have to" to one of so blessed and "get to," simply because you get to breathe air, live another day, and "get to." This is key. This change in attitude is toward the positive and helps pave the way to health and peace. You no longer live as though you "have to," but adopt a "get to" attitude instead. It is a perspective of gratitude. This coheres with the mindfulness practice of being mindful and noticing everything you do, walking, eating, or drinking tea, for example. You can take a non-judgmental attitude, which is immensely helpful, but—to some extent—this practice presupposes a positive one, gratitude. I suggest taking a positive one and trying it out.

I have heard countless people say praying with gratitude to God and thanking him has brought much blessing for them, and that their respective pain and problems seemed to subside, too, or seemingly work themselves out for the better of the person. Without the pain, one does not grow and mature, and this perspective seems to make having such problems and times more manageable. Remember, God has you exactly where God wants you—often in the midst of struggles—to learn something and grow, as rough as that can be at times. This is addressed in detail in the principle of embracing the hard times and struggles. For now, God knows exactly where you are in your life and is with you and will help with using the techniques in this chapter, especially when they are done with an eye toward God.

Since the author and readers of this are situated in the First World, it needs to be noted that here in the West, I see people lacking the proper perspective, all too often living for money, and not living for God, family, and others. Granted, we all need a certain amount of money to live and care for our families and ourselves. So many fall into the trap of, subconsciously, living for money and making it their God. They substitute this and other items, ideologies, and even vices for God, mistakenly making them into that which is to be venerated. The Buddhist approach of detachment is quite helpful on this score. It embraces watching your desire or attachments and does a great job of showing the importance of detachment and the ultimate worthlessness of attaching yourself to material things. The impermanence of existence is wisely emphasized in Buddhism as well as Hinduism, out of which the former grew.

It lays bare the fallacy that material things are valuable. There is something to be said for simplicity and minimalism, for it is the case that the more we have materially, the more problems we have. Just ask anyone who owns two houses and they will almost certainly agree that their workload and things that need to be attended to are doubled, which ultimately takes time away that could be used for more worthy, honorable, Godly pursuits. The love of money really is a form of materialism. In the end, when this life is over, we cannot take any of it with us.

Consistent with Buddhist thought, I recently saw a bumper sticker that read: "Want more, desire less." When this life is over, it will not matter how much we accumulated or how much knowledge we obtained, but rather how we loved. We can all be thankful for the gifts God has given us, while being cautious not to give them too much importance and turn them into that which we venerate. That said, gratitude is most helpful for cultivating more peace in this life.

LET GO OF GUILT AND REGRET

Guilt and regret are toxic to your body. So another technique to help cultivate peace in your life requires simply letting go of both. Remember you are forgiven by God, as all religious traditions teach, so forgive yourself. Some do not think God can forgive them or they have sinned or messed up so egregiously they cannot be forgiven or are outside God's grace—this is not the case. For such a thought presupposes their sin is bigger than God or his power to forgive and we all know that is not the case. God is omnipotent.

As noted already, we only need recall that in the Abrahamic faith traditions, God's great, paradigmatic individuals in the Hebrew Bible were fallible human beings like us. That should give us comfort. Moses committed murder, David had Uriah the Hittite sent off to the front line to die so he could have his wife (some evidence in the Hebrew text suggests he committed rape as well), and the Apostle Paul was involved with the death of Stephen because of the latter's faith in Jesus. All these men messed up royally, but later went on to be obedient to God and God used them to enact his will. God gave them grace and forgave them their sins. God does the same for each of us and most of our sins are not a big as theirs were. We should take great comfort in knowing God's paradigmatic leaders were incredibly fallible human beings, yet loved by God, forgiven and used to enact God's purpose. I wonder if that is why, in part, these stories about them, which do not paint them in a good light, are retained in the Bible: to show the magnitude of God's grace for us—God loves us completely and pardons us our transgressions. Therefore, we should forgive ourselves and not be so hard on ourselves. Doing so disrupts our peace. Remember not to judge yourself or others, as the Gospels command. Let go of toxic guilt, regret, and the sorrow that comes from them. It has recently been shown that tears of grief have toxic chemicals in them that no other human tears, like tears of joy, contain. These tears need to be released from the body as does the toxins of guilt and regret.

ADOPT A "SO WHAT?" ATTITUDE & ACT "AS IF"

"So what?" So what if you fail, so what if someone or a group does not like you, so what if you mess up a speech, so what if you make an ass of yourself? Does it really matter in the grand scheme of things? "So what" is a helpful posture and realization, as the worry is usually worse than whatever you are worrying about. In actuality, what you are concerned about rarely comes to fruition and worrying never changes the outcome, anyway—it just wreaks havoc on your body. Thus, saying "so what?" might be very helpful when you find yourself worrying about a specific thing. Adopting this attitude greatly helps alleviate worry and stress, two toxic things for us humans. On this note, Gestalt therapy advocates acting "as if." This means acting "as if" the worry is not present and this has proven a helpful approach for many. Some say, "fake it till you make it," which is really the same thing and is offered here as an example of to how to proceed after you say "so what?" to yourself. It is helpful to then "fake it until you make it" or act "as if" there is no worry. When you fake it and then keep going you find, eventually, the worry is gone and the troublesome feeling or endeavor will eventually cease to be a problem. It often becomes second nature. To some degree, this is also a form of exposure therapy and you become desensitized to the problem or issue.

EXPOSE YOURSELF TO YOUR FEAR

As intimated above, it is helpful not to avoid thoughts and settings that cause negative emotions (such as anxiety and fear), and suppress them, but rather deal with them. Exposing yourself to some level of being uncomfortable is important. For example, I used to loathe public speaking but, because of my job, I had to do it. By making myself do it and exposing myself to it, instead of avoiding it by changing jobs, I overcame it. It admittedly took a long time, years even, but finally I reached a point where I did not care nearly as much. I also let go of caring what others think of me. So, I do not care about speaking in public anymore. The ultimate remedy for the fear, counterintuitively, was being exposed to it repeatedly in order to desensitize myself to it.

Admittedly, the anxiety is not completely gone, but it is much tempered so I can function and do not get too nervous. I also control the worry or angst surrounding speaking in public with my thoughts via the CBT approach above. It might not be possible to completely eradicate all anxiety and fear surrounding certain things in life such as public speaking or going to the dentist. In fact, some anxiety is a good thing. It used to serve a biological, evolutionary purpose in warning us when danger is present. Public speaking is not dangerous, but now the anxiety might at least serve a somewhat helpful purpose in ensuring we are prepared and focused for a speaking engagement. Regardless, exposing ourselves to some degree of discomfort in life is important as running from that which we fear only makes it worse in the end, for we are running from things and afraid. Changing negative thoughts about our fears is helpful and important. Reframing from "I have to give a speech" to "I get to go through the process of giving a speech and it will allow me to get used to it and learn from it" is a more adaptive thought which does not lead to as much anxiety and as many negative consequences. Saying it will make me grow and is good exposure is a realistic and accurate way to reframe the situation.

A client once told me he was his own worst enemy and he was right. We need to analyze and be on the lookout for self-sabotaging ways of thinking and negative thoughts, in general, and change our thoughts when we notice what we are doing or when negative emotions arise. We should refer back to this chapter often when we try to ascertain which category we fall into when negative emotions and negative thoughts arise, as they go hand-in-hand. Then we should make use of the different techniques here to address our thoughts and change them to more adaptive, realistic, and accurate thoughts. Granted, it takes time, as it does to create a new habit. Experts say it takes at least two weeks to form a new habit, but when we do, we will see the change in our thoughts causes a change in our emotions which will also bring a change in our behavior. However, we can see immediately how a change in thinking can have an almost immediate and positive impact on both emotions and behaviors. For example, if you catch your thoughts when angry, it might take some time to cool down, studies show about twenty to thirty minutes, but you can have a change in behavior instantly. By catching your thoughts, you can walk away from a volatile situation instead of hitting someone, which could have far-reaching and long-lasting negative consequences. Thoughts, emotions, and behaviors are connected, so a change in one impacts the other two. We can also use watching and changing thoughts to help heal and manage many mental health issues, such as anxiety, depression, PTSD, trauma, grief, obsessive compulsive disorder, and many more. In essence, this principle of watching and altering thoughts as needed will go a very long way toward manifesting peace in anyone's life and can bring much, and even complete, healing in many instances.

Our thoughts create life or death, heaven or hell in this life. We literally make ourselves sick or make ourselves well by what we think. There is a story of a person who sought guidance and advice from the Serbian monk mentioned already in this work, Elder Thaddeus. This individual explained to Elder Thaddeus that she had an intractable problem with someone that caused much strife, something perhaps everyone can relate to. The wise monk repeated to the frustrated woman that the other individual is constantly occupying her thoughts. He further advised the woman to let the other person continue doing what she is doing. The monk then said, "Just turn your thoughts to prayer, and you will see that it will stop bothering you."[3] What profound advice for anyone and anytime regarding any problem or worry. The solution to the

3. For the story and quote, see Saint Herman of Alaska Brotherhood, *Our Thoughts Determine*, 70.

woman's problem resided in her thoughts. The monk directed her to reorient them to God and I suspect that what the monk was getting at was that all the rest would then work itself out, which it did. The monk's prescription was one that had a person engage in truly seeking first the spiritual and allowing God to take care of the all the rest (Matt 6:33). Seeking first the spiritual involves watching and altering our thoughts as needed and orienting them to what is above, God, via prayer. When this occurs, all the problems and worries in our lives are put into proper perspective and peace is manifested internally, which then radiates externally to others. Problems cease to be problems and peace very tangibly manifests.

Principle 9

Stay in the Present

Dwelling on the past brings depression and thinking about the future brings anxiety, therefore, we need to stay in the present. Otherwise, we will also miss the gift of life that is before us at the present moment. Those in the West are often caught in thoughts of the future, busying themselves trying to make money for a day that may not come. Eastern traditions do a better job of staying in the present or advocating such.

In fact, the technique of getting ourselves to stay mentally in the present has become a common intervention among therapists, particularly those who choose to intervene with the client in the realm of cognition, as opposed to behaviors or emotions. A change in one will create a change in the others. In simply telling one of my clients that staying in the past leads to depression, and the future to anxiety, I gave him an insight that caused him to catch his thoughts and redirect them to the present which, ultimately, appeared to heal him from his depression and give him a tool to use should it arise in the future.

Staying in the present as opposed to the past or the future, goes back into antiquity. The Chinese philosopher, Lao Tzu, is reported to have advocated this mental perspective. This view certainly coheres with Buddhism's principles and offers much to humanity. The use of this idea in counseling is, essentially, an appropriation of one of the foundational principles of mindfulness which comes from Eastern religious traditions—most prominently, Buddhism, specifically from Asia. Zen Buddhism does an excellent job of articulating this understanding. Its practitioners put this principle into practice via various meditation practices such as mindful eating, tea drinking, and even walking. All of these mindfulness practices have the practitioner notice and observe every little action, feeling, emotion, and so forth in the present, such as how the tea smells or tastes in a person's mouth, or what the person observes externally or internally while walking. All mindfulness observances are done in the here and now with no thoughts observing the past or future. The person is to simply be present, really present. This idea is also immensely helpful to those who struggle with post-traumatic stress disorder, particularly helping the person with it to get grounded, especially when panic or fear arises. It is also helpful for several other conditions.

Mindfulness teaches you to stay solely in the present for extended periods of time. In the present, it is worth stating again because it is so important, you are to notice every little detail of your body such as your breathing and other feelings and emotions that arise, not judging the latter or yourself when you do, irrespective of the emotions. Again, often the practice is done eating a meal, drinking a cup of tea, or going for a walk. Perhaps the best and most famous proponent of this approach or practice today is the popular Vietnamese monk, who has lived much of his life in exile and now lives in France, Thich Nhat Hanh. His books are superb and his videos can be found online detailing differing practices, such as this one. He is, without doubt, one of the foremost advocates for peace in the world today.

We Westerners can learn a lot from this practice of mindfulness and appropriate it and use it in our lives. That is why it comprises the ninth principle. It helps mental well-being and a person's peace to a great extent when utilized. Some mental health therapists even prescribe it to clients today, as the data on it shows it really works. It is a component of Eastern mindfulness practice that has been shown to have very tangible benefits for mental well-being and internal peace for those who make use of it. It is a gift from the East, notably and most prominently from Buddhist thought and practice, to the world. Granted, sustained staying in the present is not realistic or always appropriate, but it brings much relief when used throughout the day.

This notion coheres well with altering our thoughts or catching our thoughts, but it adds a new dimension if we struggle with catching and altering thoughts, as many people do. I worked with a client who had experienced much trauma and was not able to alter her negative thoughts. I presented her with the idea of acknowledging negative thoughts and saying, "Oh hi, it is you again." When she began doing it in conjunction with staying in the present it brought her much relief. DBT does a great job of integrating this acceptance technique component into a larger framework of therapy as does ACT noted in the previous chapter. You can purchase workbooks with this approach in books on DBT. In summary, do the task God places before you each day and stay in the present, not the past, as that can lead to depression, or the future, because that tends toward anxiety. Staying in the present when you feel yourself drifting toward anxiety or depression will prove very helpful, as will noticing at that point what you are feeling and thinking, without judgment, and bringing your thoughts back to the present as they start to drift to the past or future. This will go a long way toward peace.

Principle 10

Release Worry

"Do not be afraid" is the most frequently occurring line in the Bible. Pope John Paul II often noted this point during his pontificate, as he intuited a need to quell the anxiety of the modern era. He emphasized what the Bible and the ministry of Jesus tell us: that we are not to fear or worry. Mystics and spiritual giants all concur on this point. In one of her most famous poems, St. Teresa of Avila advised: "Let nothing disturb you," precisely because "All things are passing away," contrary to God who never changes. Therefore, "Whoever has God lacks nothing."

Worry and anxiety wreak havoc on the body and for all the energy they consume, ironically, they do not affect the outcome of the situation that gives rise to their presence. Worry does not help; it does quite the opposite. Worry is really useless; it does not change the outcome but instead causes much grief and unease which grows and manifests into real physical and mental ailments. A medical doctor told me the other day that 85 percent of the patients who come in to see him were really coming in because of anxiety and worry. Statistics are also showing that stress is really the root cause of many physical and mental issues that take people to a doctor. We must, therefore, find ways to release our anxieties, fears, and worries.

But how do we tangibly release worry and implore the help of the one who conquers worry and rids us of its insidious tentacles? One answer is prayer. In prayer, we can give worry over to God (see principle 7). However, this is not the only way. Following the other principles in this book will undoubtedly help, such as watching your thoughts and altering them as needed.

Research has also shown the healing, curative effects nature has. Spending time in nature, such as going for a walk, helps release anxiety. The mental benefits of gardening and how it helps facilitate the reduction of stress, anxiety, and depression is also borne out in studies. Is it any wonder, then, that when someone is in the hospital people bring flowers to them to help cheer them up? Nature is brought to them to aid in their well-being. All religious traditions hint at this and so many religious thinkers have advocated it, too. In America, the great transcendentalists, eclectically drawing from many traditions and often Hinduism, have extended meditations on God's creation, nature, and what it does to the soul when we are in nature. We need only think of Ralph Waldo Emerson's work or Henry David Thoreau and his seminal work, *Walden Pond*, published in 1854.

Having a good cry is also helpful, for it releases hormones as well as toxins from the body. Recent research has revealed that tears of joy actually differ from tears of sadness as noted already, the latter containing literal toxins that need to be purged from the body. In light of this, why would we want to hold in our tears or teach our children to do so? After all, who has not felt better after a good cry? It is important to find out what works for you, for everyone is different. We need to find what is best for ourselves in terms of self-soothing when anxiety presents itself, as some prefer to listen to soothing music to relax, others to read, write, take a bath, watch television, paint or say a rosary. Having said that, prayer or meditation and connecting to God is always helpful. On this, see the appendix *Supplication and Listening Meditation to God for Help, an Answer, or Release of a Problem to God.*

Releasing worry increases the ability to be more flexible. Being flexible allows you to go with the flow, so to speak, which increases peace and tranquility, staving off negative emotions such as irritability and frustration when things do not go as planned (which is quite often the case). Being flexible serves as a protection against emotions that disrupt peace and is, therefore, immensely important. Thus, peace and tranquility have an inverse relationship with worry, and releasing the latter is a key to manifesting peace.

OTHER HELPFUL POSTURES
IN COMBATING ANXIETY

Other practical postures can alleviate anxiety and worry, besides the obvious benefits of exercise and maintaining healthy diets for one's physical and mental well-being. Physical exercise can also be combined with a spiritual practice of prayer or meditation in a variety of ways.

Caffeine intake and sugar consumption need to be considered carefully. Caffeine is best avoided when struggling with anxiety. Excess sugar is to blame for many modern diseases. It is only now beginning to be linked to serious mental issues.

As much as possible, we should strive to be flexible and try to cultivate a laid-back attitude. Life is a gift so we should be grateful, and enjoy it. You cannot both laugh and be anxious at the same time. It has been shown scientifically that smiling improves mental well-being. We must, then, wonder whether therapists and medical doctors should prescribe a certain amount of smiling a day. Why not, if the data supports doing so and it improves mental health? Laughter, too, should possibly be prescribed. On some level, we all inherently know it has healing abilities or, at least, improves a person's mental state during (and for some time after) a good laugh. Some Indian religious traditions actually do, in fact, make simulated laughter a daily exercise; I have actually seen such in Varanasi, a most sacred city to Hindus on the Ganges River in India. Thus, go with the flow and see where God leads you. It would likely be to a better place than where you have led yourself.

It is good to recall and repeat the following words of Jesus in times of worry: "Therefore I tell you, do not worry about your life, what you will eat or what you will drink, or about your body, what you will wear. Is not life more than food and the body more than clothing?" (Matt 6:25). As confidence in life or in God's providence increases, you become more at peace. You live out the words of the Psalter: "Be still and know that I am God!" (Ps 46:10)

In whatever manner is best for you: be it exercising, catching your thoughts, going to church, saying a rosary, talking a walk, doing yoga, listening to music, reading a book, or any combination of these, make use of them to help release your anxiety and worries. Letter writing has proven helpful to many: letters to loved ones, deceased individuals, people needing forgiveness from you, or people you need to forgive. Writing a letter to help address problems—and even major trauma—can bring much healing, which also helps integrate these rough life experiences into a coherent, meaningful narrative in a person's life. Writing your life story can be very cathartic. Such integration is an important aspect of many overarching counseling theories.

Gaining a proper perspective, aided and enhanced by prayer or meditation, goes a long way in staving off worry and anxiety. Your body will tell you when it is present and time to work on dealing with it, as experience has taught all of us. As you read this, you are probably saying, "That is right, I feel the anxiety in my neck when I am overwhelmed." It seems to affect different people in different parts of the body. So often, simply having a proper mental framework staves off worry and therefore leads to better health and healing in your body, or entire being for that matter. As our bodies are temples in which the Holy Spirit dwells, we should seek to purify them of the toxins associated with worry and anxiety. Release them and manifest peace in their stead, peace for yourself and the world. As we are all intricately connected, helping ourselves manifest peace helps others manifest peace and, in turn, manifests peace for the world.

Principle 11

Find Your Meaning

Joseph Campbell famously said: "Follow your bliss." His work often pulled from the sacred texts of Hinduism, specifically the Upanishads, as it did when he formulated this simplistic yet profound statement. Bliss is unique to each person; the key is to know what your bliss is and then act on it, even if only in a partial and circumspect manner. Granted, not everyone has the luxury in this life of being able to act on their bliss or what brings them the most meaning, but chances are good you can do more than you currently are doing toward it, assuming you have even taken the time to ascertain what brings you the most meaning in life, that is, your bliss.

That what brings us meaning is important, often driving us on a subconscious level and contributing to negative emotions when stifled or ignored can be seen today in the behavior of millennials in the labor market. Arguably, this generation is just as willing to work as any other, but they are more likely to leave a job than generations prior if they do not find meaning in their job. This, at least, appears to be what the data is revealing on this specific generation. A sense of meaning appears to be the biggest factor in this generation's search for a job and contentment when already in a position.

An entire counseling theory and therapy has arisen from this idea: existential therapy. Distilled down to its essence, it is devoted to helping people find what is meaningful to them and then how to help the counselee proceed with that knowledge, as well as help with how one deals with the inescapable nature of death. It came to the fore with Viktor Frankl's book, *Man's Search for Meaning*, which details Frankl's experiences in a concentration camp under the Nazis and his subsequent work as a psychiatrist, in which he developed what is called logo therapy or meaning therapy.[1] Frankl's work revealed how he found meaning in the direst of circumstances and how those who had no reason to live were the ones who did not make it under the horrific circumstances of the Shoah. His book is a firsthand account of how having a sense of purpose helps us live.

Existential therapy also arises out of the thought of existentialist philosophers, starting with Soren Kierkegaard. Today, it is associated most with its most prolific expounder and writer of the therapy, Irvin Yalom. He is the best known proponent of it today. All exponents do seem to maintain the same thing—meaning is derived from the individual, not an outside source, and it is important for various reasons, such as a person's happiness and sense of purpose in life. The therapy aims to help one find out what that specific meaning is for each person. When we uncover it and act upon it even to a small degree, we live a more fulfilled and meaningful life, one in which we have more peace and well-being because we know we have a purpose and a meaning. The data shows when we think or feel this way we actually have better health. Thus, finding meaning is vital for peace and one of the twelve principles.

As noted, meaning is not derived from outside, but from within. The locus of control is internal with regard to meaning. For a great many, including the present author, meaning is derived from an outward source but is adopted internally. Thus, for many, God is the outward that is internally adopted to create meaning. I could even say in the Christian tradition, the Holy Spirit inside is what gives meaning to life. Admittedly, for many, God is not

1. Frankl, *Man's Search*, 103–36.

what brings meaning. What is argued here is that, whatever it is, we need to find what brings us specific meaning or bliss in life and act on it to whatever degree, if possible.

Whatever it is, living with a sense of purpose and meaning brings health and longevity. Again, meaning is different for everyone, for some it is incorporating or living according to a religious tradition, such as Catholicism, and that ultimately provides meaning to that person. Often, it is in part or entirely aligned with the meaning your religious tradition provides, and there is nothing wrong with that. It may be you are a Catholic and the partaking of the Eucharist or adoration is ultimately what brings you meaning in life. I have seen what engaging in the Eucharist and adoration frequently and reverently can do for someone who values it, and the amazing transformative power it brings those who find it meaningful. For others, it is being the best at their career; for some, it is raising a family, bodybuilding, running, writing, helping a friend over coffee with spiritual/existential struggles, or just being more informed about the world around them and social issues. Everyone is different and that difference is how God created us; our differences are a gift.

It could be argued that we need to make sure our perspective and meaning are rightly placed, but in reality, for health and happiness, we need only find what is meaningful to us and then do things toward that end. Not to mention that being "rightly placed," in regards to what is meaningful for us, is rather subjective. We will be surprised how it impacts and often reorients life for the better when we labor under an understanding, even a very vague one, that our lives have meaning and we are acting in alignment with that meaning. I have noticed that when one acts contrary to what they find meaningful, or their beliefs, it creates an enormous amount of internal conflict and cognitive dissonance, as noted already. It usually makes people end up in my office.

Finding meaning is immensely important and brings true contentment in life. Happiness comes from it—though happiness is a transient state, not sustained for terribly long increments. Once your meaning is found, which merely takes sitting down and doing some introspection, the part that is vital is acting on it, either in your leisure time, at work, or in how you interact with your family. Anything counts, even if it is only by giving the pursuit a few hours in your week, such as tutoring a person in need or volunteering at a homeless shelter an hour a week. It is important to note that it is not realistic to expect every aspect of your life to be meaningful. You should not presume that to be possible. It is the human condition that we must till the ground (Gen 3) and engage in tasks we would rather not do to survive—but the mundane tasks likely have as much to teach us as our more lofty endeavors, just at the struggles do.

For some people, meaning is based on achievement, meaningful relationships, belonging, and for many (of course), making money. I once had a friend say, when I asked about what ultimately brought him meaning, "to make money." He was honest, but I must admit he is not happy today. In the end, this might be a more shallow pursuit than most realize; we never feel fulfilled or that we ultimately have enough. Though subjective, I would argue, true meaning cannot be found in it. To be blunt, it does need to be stated here that, especially since the context of the writer and reader of this book is the Western First World, the author's view is that money does not bring authentic happiness or peace. Studies have shown this, provided one has enough to live on for survival. As stated already several times in this work, true, lasting peace and happiness come from God, not anything else, such as money, fame, respect, substances, or even another person.

The sentiment touched on already and associated with St. Francis of Assisi, though augmented and expanded by my own words, needs to be mentioned here again as some reading this are likely searching in their minds for what brings them meaning and even likely are wanting to find a new meaning or bliss to internalize and follow. When this life is over and we are all standing before the transcendent, it will not matter how much we have accumulated or even how much we know, but rather how we loved that counts. This, I believe, is what truly matters and a bliss worth following, though the present author is dangerously close to pushing his agenda on the reader and what he thinks is more meaningful, an unethical move for a therapist, no doubt—though this, technically, is not therapy. That said, ultimately what is suggested here is that we find our specific meaning and act upon it, no matter how small a gesture.

At the very least, finding your meaning in life will lead to you being more occupied. People enjoy spending time in such endeavors that bring them meaning. In short, it keeps someone busy, and being active is known to have much better health benefits than a sedentary lifestyle. The busier a person is, oftentimes, the healthier. That is why when people retire, their health often, regrettably, goes downhill if they do not take up hobbies and projects that get them involved mentally, emotionally, and physically. It is important to stay active. Without activity and meaning we tend to go downhill.

Ironically, those who are busiest end up being the ones who when given an additional hard project, get it done. This is not necessarily someone who has more time on their hands. A look at the desks of the world's most famous individuals shows that they are the messiest and this suggests the busiest. The greatest thinkers and most prolific writers, such as Sigmund Freud, Albert Einstein, Karl Barth, Leo Tolstoy, among many others, all worked exceedingly long hours, some eighteen hours a day, infused with a sense of meaning derived from their work. One could argue they all changed the world in many ways.

A study revealed that several nuns had Alzheimer's disease, but they did not display any symptoms of the disease. They did not suffer the effects of the debilitating disease because they stayed very busy. It needs to be emphasized that, at the time of having the sinister disease, they all had a sense of purpose and meaning in life. Many with the disease occupied their time and derived great meaning at this phase in their life by doing for others as they could. Many of the nuns would drive the other older nuns to and from doctors' appointments and many would even still teach classes to the other nuns and outsiders. They stayed busy with a sense of purpose. Their sense of meaning derived from taking care of others and doing the work God placed before them in the latter years of their lives. This appears to have staved off the effects of Alzheimer's disease for each of the nuns. Acting upon what brought meaning in their lives likely lengthened their lives. It is interesting to note that their sense of meaning was also infused with—or could be understood in large measure—as living to serve God, God's creation, and humanity. Finding meaning and acting upon it is thus a way to prolong your life or, at least, make the quality of your life better, not all that different than some medications.

Can a doctor prescribe finding your meaning? In a way, that is precisely what the main aspect of existential therapy attempts to do. As these nuns reveal, finding purpose and meaning most likely even prolongs life. It also suggests doing so has a way of working against negative thoughts and maladies or unease. Rather, finding meaning allows peace to manifest. Finding and acting upon what brings you meaning in life, however unique it may be, is vitally important and brings wholeness, health, contentment, thus *shalom* or peace.

This understanding is also applicable to romantic relationships. You need to understand what brings meaning in life to you and your partner, assuming one has a partner, and this is not to suggest being single is a bad thing. Many people are perfectly happy single. One major element that contributes to a successful marriage is understanding what brings each partner meaning. Meaning is different for all of us, and knowing what brings your partner meaning can truly help a marriage, aiding you in your efforts to better understand a partner and what drives them. To know how your partner derives meaning is helpful for your relationship and is good common sense. The more you know about your partner, the better you can help them, align with them, show empathy and understanding, and navigate difficult terrain.[2]

To be fair, not everyone has the luxury of pursuing that which brings them the most meaning in their lives or what gives them purpose. This luxury, however, is not the privilege of the affluent; most of us in the West irrespective of our socioeconomic status can find some time to peruse what brings meaning. I know of one

2. See Gottman and Silver, *Seven Principles.*

person who has a very successful job that he does not like. He cannot leave in part because, financially, he could not find another job and must support his family. To some extent, this contributes to symptoms of depression, manifested by anger. After some therapy, this conflict was resolved by the individual finding a hobby he loved that brought him meaning. This satisfied a deep need and peace returned to the man. A hobby can thus be the manner in which a person finds and acts upon what is meaningful and individually specific to them. I would venture to say that if his wife and family supported his hobby, out of an awareness of the importance of everyone being allowed to find and enact this principle, an even higher level of peace and cohesiveness in his home life would be obtained, a peace for the individual that exudes into the entire family structure and beyond.

PRINCIPLE 12

Acknowledge and Embrace Hard Times and Struggles

STRUGGLES ARE A PART of life. Their presence does not necessarily mean things have gone wrong. They are to be expected, even welcomed, for without them we do not mature. Life is something none of us will get out of alive and we will all collect a significant amount of scars as we journey through it. Richard Rohr, the famous Franciscan author and mystic, explained that the "refusal of the necessary pain of being human brings to the person ten times more suffering in the long run."[1]

Total freedom from strife and hardships is not possible this side of heaven, thus sustained peace, lasting all of life, is not possible. Strife is a part of life but we can, in fact, have peace during the strife. When we realize that problems and struggles coming and going is a part of life, not a punishment from God or an aberration, we can more readily embrace them when they arise and learn from them. They will then often prove to be rather fleeting and we will not be so discombobulated and uneasy when they arrive. The Bible tells us, "whenever you face trials of any kind, consider it nothing

1. Rohr, *Falling Upward*, 73.

but joy, because you know that the testing of your faith produces endurance" (Jas 1:2).

According to James, those who persevere under trial will receive the crown of life (Jas 1:12). This is not what we naturally think when trials and problems arise, especially when they are big or extreme ones. Eastern religious traditions, particularly mindfulness practices, have pointed out that instead of ignoring problems, it is often important to acknowledge their presence and impact on our lives. It is important to implicitly see and almost embrace them, instead of ignoring or fighting against them. Both Western and Eastern traditions agree on the value of trials.

The pastor Rick Warren noted in *The Purpose Driven Life* that at any one time in a person's life not all aspects of their life will be what they desire. There will always be a problem present, so we must learn to be content in spite of that fact. Things at work might be going wonderfully, but a mess at home is present or vice versa. Warren has had to deal with the loss of a child. It is impossible to be free from struggles and a lot of them are often present at once. It is part of the ebb and flow of life. Things will never be perfect; this life is not supposed to be. The secret is learning how to be content and find peace in spite of what is transpiring around you or happening to you. Learning to be peaceful and joyful in the little graces life has to offer during the mundane and normal, as well as in the storms, is key.

In the last book he wrote, Henri Nouwen articulated the paradox of suffering with the metaphor of the cup Jesus had to drink. This "cup of sorrow, inconceivable as it seems, is also the cup of joy. Only when we consider this in our own life can we consider drinking it."[2] Indeed, good fruits may result from some of our sorrows—for instance, when we reorient our lives to God, are purified of certain things, our lives are turned in a different direction, or we meet someone we otherwise never would have met. Granted, it is hard to see how cancer or the death of a loved one can do this, but if we look deep enough into the darkness, we might find some

2. Nouwen and Anderson, *Can You Drink?*, 43.

good: "When we are crushed like grapes, we cannot think of the wine we will become."[3]

Ronald Rolheiser maintains that, in this life, we never fully satisfy our desires and needs, so we must learn to deal with loss in all forms: loved ones, health, jobs, dreams, loves, fulfilled wishes, etc. We all have things left undone. In fact, the second half of life is learning to deal with death, the death of our dreams, loved ones, health, jobs, marriages, and so forth. Resolving our losses is the key to living according to the Easter mystery, a model applicable to any type of loss or death in this life:[4]

- Good Friday: name your deaths
- Easter Sunday: claim your births
- Forty Days: grieve what you have lost and adjust to the new reality
- Ascension: do not cling to the old, let it ascend and give you its blessing
- Pentecost: accept the new spirit for the new life you have

Rolheiser is not a pessimist. If we know suffering is a natural part of life, and even embrace it for the blessing it brings instead of running from it, we will have more peace in life. Happy is the person who has learned to be happy in spite of disappointment and the inevitable losses in life. Again, the secret is to learn to be thankful and appreciate what we do have in spite of everything else. We must mourn our loss before being reborn into a new life. After adequate time, we are born into a new way of living, one that understands we need to learn how to live and be happy in spite of the deaths we have had, and to appreciate the gifts life still has to offer. We thus have a proper perspective. For example, instead of waking up and saying, "My loved one is gone and my body is sick," we say, "I am grateful for this day, that I had years with a person, and that I am still alive and given another day." Another case of reframing.

---

3. Nouwen and Anderson, *Can You Drink?*, 54.
4. Rolheiser, *Holy Longing*, 141–66.

Voltaire supposedly once said, "Life is a shipwreck, but we must not forget to sing in the lifeboats."[5] Though his overall view is grim, he is onto something. Though I do not think he would see eye-to-eye with many of us, perhaps his sentiment betrays an understanding of the gift of life that invites us to sing in the lifeboat. Perhaps the biggest comfort we can have after the death of a loved one is the hope that death is not the end (according to our faith traditions). Our loved ones live on in our memories and we will be reunited with them one day.

Every single day is a gift. Every breath we take is a gift from God. How many of us are thankful for that or think in these terms? We perhaps assume it is a right and things should be a certain way; in this, we are mistaken. We need be thankful we get to breathe today and have another day on this earth, or that we get one more sunset in this life, or one more visit with a loved one or friend. We forget to see the blessings we do get and life is that—a blessing. It is about perspective. If we reframe and remind ourselves of this fact, happiness and a little more peace will manifest. What a change would happen in the world, on a global level and on an individual level, if such a perspective were cultivated. Perspective is thus key for manifesting peace, as previously discussed in chapter 8. Though pithy, it is nonetheless the case that we do not know the good without the bad. This perspective is but another way to help mitigate against despair in bad times, as well as saying to ourselves, "This, too, shall pass," for time does bring healing, admittedly not as fast as we desire.

The famous medieval historian C. S. Lewis said, "Pain is God's megaphone to rouse a deaf world."[6] This pain, in turn, reorients us to God and makes our focus go upward. Fumbling in life, embarrassing moments, heartaches, suffering, or pain of any sort is inevitable and should be welcomed to some extent for they are opportunities to learn. Without them, we would not grow. We learn about ourselves in the process and if we learn and listen to

5. In fact, this is a interpretation of the end of Voltaire's *Candide* by Gay, *Enlightenment*, 201.

6. Lewis, *Problem of Pain*, 91.

the wisdom to be gleaned from our trials and tribulations, we learn where our true refuge and source lies, as does our next breath—in God. Richard Rohr's *Falling Upward* opens by reminding its readers of the wisdom of Julian of Norwich when she wrote, "First there is the fall, then we recover from the fall. Both are the mercy of God!"

A veteran student in one of my Introduction to Religious Studies class told a fellow friend struggling with PTSD that the way he got over things, and the way the friend should, was simply to accept the negative thoughts. Do not try to ignore them. He intuitively knew this would make stuff fester inside. We need to get it out, just as we need to cry when things are bad. Tears of grief, as previously noted, have been shown to contain toxins, whereas happy tears do not. This reveals the need to cry to, quite literally, get the toxins out of our systems. Our bodies are truly remarkable and created in the image of God (Gen 1:27). This vet was telling a friend to recognize the thoughts and not reject them. He was also aware that it is better to deal with painful thoughts, memories, and the like than it is to bottle them up. He inherently knew dealing with them is better and understood the importance of exposure therapy (in small, manageable dosages) after someone has the requisite skills to deal with the thoughts and settings that cause problems. This then desensitizes a person to the negative thoughts so that they, eventually, are no longer bothersome to the person. He knew avoidance of the thoughts, memories, or settings that trigger either perpetuated the problems for people battling PTSD. He realized the start to healing was recognizing the thoughts and emotions and accepting them—not judging them by simply, counterintuitively, accepting them. A caveat is important here. If you feel you have PTSD, or have been through trauma in the past, it is better to work with a therapist. They will be trained in how to help you deal with PTSD properly, especially the exposure therapy elements. Exposure therapy needs to occur under the guidance of a trained professional. Additionally, eye movement desensitization and reprocessing therapy (EMDR) has proven immensely helpful for PTSD cases and is being used with success for everything from anxiety and depression to trauma and chronic pains. Whereas medications (e.g. the standard regiment of an SSRI and a Benzodiazepine to address anxiety) treat the symptoms, in theory EMDR treats the root of the problem, often a traumatic event, with remarkable results. In essence, this wise veteran correctly told his friend to say, "Oh, hey there, it is you again" to negative thoughts, feelings, and struggles, free of any judgment. This is the start to healing and a mindfulness approach that the Sufi mystic, Rumi, advocated in the most eloquent of terms years ago. Countless people through the ages and countless people alive today have found great solace in the poem.

As C.S. Lewis intimated, pain induces theological reflection. We start, at least, to think about God. On a collective scale, a historical example can be seen with the kingdom of Judah being conquered by the Neo-Babylonians and its inhabitants being hauled off into exile after their temple was destroyed. This ushered in a time of great suffering and anguish, not to mention a great amount of cognitive dissonance. It caused enormous theological reflection among the people, as the people wanted to know why God allowed such a calamity. An explanation was sought, after much reflection, and can be found throughout the pages of the Hebrew Bible. God allowed it because the people had gone astray in worshipping other gods and needed to return to God. It was immensely painful, but the suffering inflicted had a purpose no one could see at the time, a purpose that served a larger and more important end.

Life indeed is wonderful, but it is also really hard and painful. Both are necessary, for we cannot truly know one without the other, as noted above. Both are always present. Said differently, it takes the bad to know the good in life and the good to know the bad. Both also bring lessons to learn. That both bad and good are always present, though the extent of each ebbs and flows, is known to all on some level when genuinely reflecting on our lives. Things might be going very well, but joy is tempered by pain and sadness, just as pain and sadness are always offset by some measure of joy. Sometimes in the pain we only have the joy of the presence of a friend or smile of a loved one, but this is some measure of joy.

There is always a silver lining. Joys and pains are intertwined in our lives and ever-present. We need to resolve the pains to the best of our ability in order to live in peace with the heartaches, knowing joy is present, too.

A physician once said that sickness is a beautiful gift; it very often comes to teach us something and, when we have learned the lesson, the teacher departs. Undoubtedly, it is when we have the ability to look back that we can take this approach.

To be fair, pain and suffering are not inherently good. Some trials push people over the edge permanently. One should never seek to explain evil and justify it. The point here is that good can come out of suffering if we manage to find the strength to face it and deal with it until it serves a didactic purpose to transform us.

DOUBT AND FAITH IN THE STRUGGLES

Life is wonderful and can be horrible as well. It takes the bad to know the good, as noted, and this has, perhaps, become a cliché. The techniques in this book are intended to help navigate life. Sometimes misfortune occurs, but the sun will rise again—if not in this life, in the next. If the worst has happened, know death is not the end, and you will be reunited with your loves ones. We are only here but for the blink of an eye when compared to eternity and death is not the end. Life is hard, exceedingly so at times, but the hard times and struggles will one day give rise to the dawn.

You need also not be hard on yourself if faith is a struggle and you often do not believe in God. Doubt is a natural part of authentic faith. This is something that is rarely talked about, and likely denied by some, though nonetheless true. Faith, oftentimes, entails getting out of bed and continuing in spite of times when you do not really believe, which comes to all people of mature faith if they are honest with themselves and others.

Numerous commendable and faith-filled individuals worthy of admiration experienced this reality. C.S. Lewis is one example as he struggled immensely with despair and doubt following the death of his beloved, Joy Davidman. Many readers will also be familiar with Mother Teresa's "Dark Night of the Soul" experience, which lasted several decades, in which she felt God was absent or silent and in which she, oftentimes, found herself bereft of faith. Throughout history many of these individuals experienced such times. Their experiences served, ultimately, to grow each in their faiths. It is also important to note that many, including St. Francis of Assisi and Ignatius of Loyola, suffered immense physical ailments for a season that almost took their lives, but these experiences would serve as a catalyst for a life devoted to God.

Solace and consolation for us today can be found, and have been found for those voices of the past who are no longer with us, in the fact that times of doubt, spiritual dryness, and even despair are not the last word. Eventually, the dawn comes. For most of us, dawn will arise in this life; unfortunately, for some, it will be in the life to come. The good news is that it will come and last throughout eternity. The dawn will come for all precisely because of the person and work of Jesus the Christ, according to Christians. His atoning work on the cross does not make death the last word, rather it provides hope—a hope that we can cling to joyfully during good times, but all the more so in times of doubt and despair.

Our times of doubt or pain serve as desert times in our lives when God is working on our soul. Granted, we would prefer to have these times pass us by, but oftentimes these experiences serve to reorient ourselves toward God. Being in the midst of such trials provides us with an opportunity to mature and grow in ways imperceptible to us while they are occuring. As Paul maintained: "For now we see in a mirror, dimly" (1 Cor 13:12). We might not understand why we suffer, but we can at least hold on to the knowledge that times of pain and hardship often bring about a purification and sanctification of our souls.

Catholic tradition has done a wonderful job of articulating the notion that we should offer up our pain to God and suffer for God just as God, according to Christians, suffered for us. Those who undertake suffering in such a manner are often blessed, and frequently reveal how God worked through them during their dark days, sometimes even touching the lives of others in very positive ways due to their hardships. This reality can allow us to be happy in the midst of our suffering as happiness is often a choice. In Judaism, happiness is actually a commandment. In the video, *Catholicism: The Pivotal Players, Vol. I*, Bishop Robert Barron argues that becoming holy or leading an authentic religious life is about dying to self, releasing or giving up the desires of the ego. Such a dying to self then allows a person to be more connected to God. Thus God lives in us, as the apostle Paul explains, and God's will is enacted, not ours. However, this process hurts and causes suffering, as in choosing God and dying to self we give up some deep desires and wants.

The delightful movie, *The Best Exotic Marigold Hotel*, set in Jaipur, India contains a memorable quote: "Everything will be alright in the end, so if it is not alright, it is not the end." If you are in turmoil or doubt, however difficult it is, try to remember it is not the end. There can be blessing in a person's suffering. Sometimes all we can do is just keep going forward, however small the increments might be. It becomes an act of faith, a faith that contends in its action that God will pave the way and that the present suffering is not the end.

Conclusion

THE TWELVE PRINCIPLES PRESENTED here have the potential to manifest peace in your life. Many more principles and techniques could be added, however, the twelve detailed are the salient ones for obtaining more peace here and now. They can bring fast relief, given some effort and regularity in practice. By now, the reader will have gleaned a few subthemes running throughout this work— ones that, in themselves, could even be understood as additional principles. They are postures with which to view the world and life, and thus, perspectives that help us better implement the twelve principles.

One of the most important decisions a person can make is whether to live in faith or in fear. Fear slowly destroys while faith sustains and even heals. When we proceed from faith, the results are nothing short of amazing. It does not mean life will always be easy, but we have the assurance God is with us and that we can have peace, even in the midst of intense struggles. As Paul wrote to the Philippians, this peace surpasses all understanding, and that very peace is what guards both our hearts and our minds (Phil 4:7).

The twelve principles advocated here are no miraculous receipts to a blissful life. They only produce change if implemented. Besides the necessary effort to practice them, some discernment is required to find out which principle is appropriate to your specific situation and which ones work best for you.

These principles are not new. Religious traditions and philosophical systems have advocated them since their inception. Virtually every culture has advocated forms of each principle. Psychology and counselling simply appropriated them. What is new here is how these universally accepted practices and wisdom teachings are presented through the lens of a faith perspective, most often a Christian one. However, it has been seen that all can profit from making use of these principles regardless of their religious or non-religious tradition. These principles are tried and proven approaches to garner peace in one's life.

Who could not make do with more peace, as life is naturally hard and stressful at times? These principles offer tangible ways to more peace, well-being, healing, and wholeness. The appendices at the end of this book contain numerous prayer and meditation exercises to help you come closer to God, forgive others, or discern what to do in a particular situation. It is my earnest prayer that these principles, informed by religious traditions, spiritual individuals, psychology, and, dare I say, God will help you in your journey toward manifesting peace.

Appendix A

Summary of the Twelve Principles

- Principle 1: *Let Go of Caring What Others Think of You*
- Principle 2: *Let Go of the Need to Be Right*
- Principle 3: *Refrain from Assumptions*
- Principle 4: *Suspend all Judgment and Let Others Live Their Lives*
- Principle 5: *Maintain Healthy Boundaries*
- Principle 6: *Forgive*
- Principle 7: *Meditate and Connect to God*
- Principle 8: *Watch and Alter Thoughts as Needed*
- Principle 9: *Stay in the Present*
- Principle 10: *Release Worry*
- Principle 11: *Find Your Meaning*
- Principle 12: *Acknowledge and Embrace Hard Times and Struggles*

APPENDIX B

Spirituality Practices for Peace

EACH PRACTICE BELOW SHOULD, ideally, be done for a minimum of twenty minutes a day, but you can start with ten minutes a day and increase it as you go.

CONNECTING TO GOD MEDITATION

- Sit either in a comfortable chair or on the ground in lotus position or with legs crossed.
- Gently and slowly take three deep breaths.
- Orientate your mind to God (you could repeat the Jesus prayer three times).
- Become still and quiet and focus your attention on your breathing for a few minutes.
- Then let your mind choose to focus on nothing.
- As thoughts come to your mind, do not judge them or your-self, but simply turn them over to God and let them gently leave your mind (you could imagine each thought as a balloon that flies away).

- Try to do this for at least twenty minutes. Afterwards, you can say a prayer to conclude the session (the Lord's prayer, if you so choose).

SIMPLE MEDITATION

- Sit either in a comfortable chair or on the ground in lotus position or with legs crossed.
- Gently and slowly take three deep breaths.
- Become still and quiet and focus your attention on your breathing for a few minutes.
- Then let your mind choose to focus on nothing.
- As thoughts come to your mind, do not judge them or yourself, but simply let them gently leave your mind (you could imagine each thought as a balloon that flies away).

A minimum of twenty minutes is recommended.

MEDITATION PRAYING WITH SCRIPTURE

- Gently and slowly take three deep breaths.
- Orientate your mind to God.
- Engage in a gratitude prayer, thanking God for all your specific blessings.
- Open the Bible or another spiritual source and read the spiritual text slowly.
- Listen to your intuition, inner voice, or the Spirit for what stands out to you.
- Close the book and your eyes and focus on what stands out to you.
- As your mind wanders, bring it back to what you have been led to focus on.

- Do this for fifteen to twenty minutes and see what else arises in regards to the text you are focusing on.

- Close with a prayer, then open your eyes.

SUPPLICATION AND LISTENING MEDITATION TO GOD FOR HELP, AN ANSWER, OR RELEASE OF A PROBLEM TO GOD

- Sit either in a comfortable chair or on the ground in lotus position or with legs crossed.

- Gently and slowly take three deep breaths.

- Orientate your mind to God (you could repeat the Jesus prayer three times).

- Become still and quiet and focus your attention on your breathing for a few minutes.

- Then let your mind choose to focus on God.

- Offer a brief prayer of gratitude for all that God has done for you and provided for you.

- Be still for a little while in awe of God and praise God for who God is and for having created you and all of creation.

- Gently tell God you are listening and ask God to speak to you; you can ask for help or an answer to a specific issue or for insight, as well as the ability to forgive someone; essentially, you can ask God for help with anything and release a particular problem to God at this time. You can turn your fears or worries over to God.

- Listen in silence for what comes to you. You have done the talking/asking of God, now it is time to sit in silence and listen to the language of God, silently, patiently.

- Enjoy the time and let it recharge you.

A minimum of twenty minutes is recommended. Afterwards, you can say a prayer to conclude the session.

Appendix B

MEDITATION FOR LOVE OR FORGIVENESS

- Sit in a room and concentrate on your breathing.

- Still your mind.

- Think of someone you love, something you love to do, or a place that makes you very happy and at peace.

- Once you have noticed a happy, positive feeling in your body and how it spreads throughout your whole body, allow yourself to sit in that positive feeling of love for awhile so it can impact your whole body and being.

- After some time, substitute the person you need to forgive with the previous thing that brought love to your being. Stay with the positive feeling for them as long as it lasts. If you do not need to forgive someone, you can simply remain in the positive state and let it continue to impact your whole being for around twenty minutes.

- If you have substituted a person in your mind you need to forgive, when the positive emotions and feelings dissipate, go back to the other image of the person or place you love for a time, allowing the positive feelings of love to arise again, before repeating the substitution for the one you need to forgive. Repeat this exercise a few times before concluding.

ANOTHER MEDITATION FOR INSIGHT ON AN ISSUE

- Gratitude prayer.

- Watch breathing.

- Pray for insight and ask God for illumination.

- Sit and breathe.

- Contemplate the issue from multiple vantage points—often from the other person's perspective, if you are dealing with another person and an issue surrounding them. Also ask and observe to see how something in their past is affecting the way they are acting. Do not judge the other person, rather, have complete compassion for them. You will see that you are connected to them and everyone else.

MEDITATION ON A SACRED WORD OR IMAGE

This one is great for relief from anxiety or depression and reorienting your life to God.

- Sit either in a comfortable chair or on the ground in lotus position or with legs crossed.
- Gently and slowly take three deep breaths.
- Orientate your mind to God (you could repeat the Jesus prayer three times).
- Become still and quiet and focus your attention on your breathing for a few minutes.
- Then let your mind choose to focus on a sacred word, phrase, or image, such as Jesus healing the leper in the Gospels or the Virgin Mary.
- Say the sacred word over and over again or hold the picture of the image in your mind.
- When your mind wanders or other thoughts arise, gently let them go and refocus on the sacred item(s) of your choice.

A minimum of twenty minutes is recommended.

VISUALIZATION EXERCISE

This one can be used for healing or to enhance performance. One minute after you wake up and before you go to bed at night, visualize or picture, in detail, the life you desire. This may also be done during meditation/prayer and mindfulness practice.

GUIDED IMAGERY FOR HEALING

- Sit either in a comfortable chair or on the ground in lotus position or with legs crossed.

- Gently and slowly take three deep breaths.

- Orientate your mind to God (you could repeat the Jesus prayer three times).

- Become still and quiet and focus your attention on your breathing for a few minutes.

- Then let your mind choose that part of the body you want to be healed.

- Focus your attention on the healing power of God coming into your body and then going to that part you want healed. Visualize that part of the body healing in great detail, even down to the cells being restored and healed. Proceed slowly through the entire region you want healed. It might be the entire body. You can picture white light penetrating the cells, tissues, muscles, or organs and then moving around the desired region. Some picture white healing energy coming into the body via each inhaled breath and toxins leaving the body via the exhale.

- Do this for fifteen minutes every day for a minimum of two weeks, though doing it for a longer period of time is best, and see what happens.

Bibliography

Anderson, James. *Extolling Yeshua*. Eugene: Wipf & Stock,. Forthcoming.

Bacovcin, Helen. *The Way of a Pilgrim and the Pilgrim Continues His Way: A New Translation*. Garden City, NY: Image, 1978.

Beck, Judith S. *Cognitive Behavior Therapy: Basics and Beyond*. New York: Guilford, 2011.

Bengt, Runo Hoffman. *The Theologia Germanica of Martin Luther*. Classics of Western Spirituality. New York: Paulist, 1980.

Bennett, John G. and Manandhar, T. L. *Long Pilgrimage: The Life and Teachings of the Shivapuri Baba*. Clearlake, CA: The Drawn Horse, 1975.

Blum, Jason N. *Zen and the Unspeakable God: Comparative Interpretations of Mystical Experience*. University Park, PA: Penn State University Press, 2015.

Charlesworth, James H. and Loren L. Johns, eds. *Hillel and Jesus: Comparative Studies of Two Major Religious Leaders*. Minneapolis: Fortress, 1997.

Chitakure, John. *The Pursuit of the Sacred: An Introduction to Religious Studies*. Eugene, OR: Wipf & Stock, 2016.

Chopra, Deepak. *Ageless Body, Timeless Mind: A Practical Alternative to Growing Old*. London: Random House, 2003.

Chumley, Norris. *Mysteries of the Jesus Prayer: Experiencing the Mysteries of God and a Pilgrimage to the Heart of an Ancient Spirituality*. New York: HarperCollins, 2011.

Cook, William R. *Francis of Assisi: The Way of Poverty and Humility*. Eugene, OR: Wipf & Stock, 2008.

Dispenza, Joe. *You Are the Placebo: Making Your Mind Matter*. Carlsbad, CA: Hay House, 2014.

Farasiotis, Dionysios and Philip Navarro. *The Gurus, the Young Man, and Elder Paisios*. Platina, CA: St. Herman, 2008.

Frankl, Viktor E. *Man's Search for Meaning*. New York: Simon & Schuster, 1985.

Gay, Peter. *The Enlightenment: An Interpretation*. New York: Knopf, 1966.

Gottman, John and Nan Silver. *The Seven Principles for Making Marriage Work: A Practical Guide from the Country's Foremost Relationship Expert*. New York: Harmony, 2015.

Bibliography

Hahn, Thich Naht. *Being Peace*. Berkeley: Parallax, 1987.

Hipolito, E. et al. "Trauma-Informed Care: Accounting for the Interconnected Role of Spirituality and Empowerment in Mental Health Promotion." *Journal of Spirituality in Mental Health* 16 (2014) 193–217.

Jorgensen, Johannes. *Saint Catherine of Siena*. Eugene, OR: Wipf & Stock, 2012.

Julian of Norwich. *Revelations of Divine Love*. Translated by Elizabeth Spearing. Penguin Classics. London: Penguin. 1998.

Keating, Thomas. *Intimacy with God: An Introduction to Centering Prayer*. New York: Crossroad, 2009.

————. *Manifesting God*. New York: Lantern, 2005.

Kerr, Michael E., and Murray Bowen. *Family Evaluation*. New York: Norton, 1988.

Leaf, Caroline. *Switch On Your Brain: The Key to Peak Happiness, Thinking, and Health*. Grand Rapids: Baker, 2013.

Lewis, Clive Staples. *The Problem of Pain*. San Francisco: Harper, 2001.

Luther, Martin. *The Theologia Germanica of Martin Luther*. Classics of Western Spirituality. Edited and translated by Bengt Hoffmann. Mahwah, NJ: Paulist, 1980.

Matthews, Warren. *World Religions*. 3rd ed. Belmont: Wadsworth Publishing Company, 1999.

Merton, Thomas. *The Asian Journal of Thomas Merton*. New York: New Directions, 1975.

————. *Conjectures of a Guilty Bystander*. Garden City, NY: Doubleday, 1966.

————. *The Seven Storey Mountain*. Wilmington, MA: Houghton Mifflin Harcourt, 1999.

————. *The Waters of Siloe*. San Diego: A Harvest Book; Harcourt Brace & Company, 1979.

Murdock, Nancy L. *Theories of Counseling and Psychotherapy: A Case Approach*. 3rd ed. Upper Saddle River, NJ: Pearson, 2013.

Nouwen, Henri J. M., and Dan Anderson. *Can You Drink the Cup?* Notre Dame, IN: Ave Maria, 1996.

Peale, Norman Vincent. "Thought Conditioners: Forty Powerful Spiritual Phrases that Can Change the Quality of your Life." http://gaurang.org/pub/thought-conditioners-norman-vincent-peale.pdf.

Pennington, M. Basil. *Thomas Merton: My Brother: His Journey to Freedom, Compassion and Final Integration*. New York: New City, 1996.

Rohr, Richard. *Falling Upward: A Spirituality for the Two Halves of Life*. San Francisco: Jossey-Bass, 2011.

Rolheiser, Ronald. *The Holy Longing: The Search for a Christian Spirituality*. New York: Doubleday, 1999.

————. *Prayer: Our Deepest Longing*. Cincinnati, OH: Franciscan Media, 2013.

Ruiz, Don Miguel and Janet Mills. *The Four Agreements: A Practical Guide to Personal Freedom*, vol. 1. San Rafael, CA: Amber-Allen, 2010.

Bibliography

Rumi, Jalal al-Din. *The Essential Rumi*. Translated by Coleman Barks. Edison, NJ: Castle, 1997.

Saint Augustine. *Saint Augustine: Confessions*. Translated by Henry Chadwick. Oxford: Oxford University Press, 1991.

Saint Herman of Alaska Brotherhood. *Our Thoughts Determine Our Lives: The Life and Teachings of Elder Thaddeus of Vitovnica*. Translated by Ana Smiljanic. Platina, CA: Saint Herman, 2015.

Salinger, Jerome David, Annemarie Böll, and Heinrich Böll. *Franny and Zooey*. Boston: Little & Brown, 1961.

St. John of the Cross *Dark Night of the Soul*. London: Penguin, 2003.

Tetlow, Joseph A. *Making Choices in Christ*. Chicago: Loyola, 2008.

Thoreau, Henry David. *Walden*. New Haven: Yale University Press, 2006.

Thoresen, Carl E., Alex H. S. Harris, and Frederic Luskin. *Forgiveness and Health: An Unanswered Question*. New York: Guilford, 2000.

Warren, Rick. *The Purpose Driven Life: What on Earth am I Here For?* Grand Rapids: Zondervan, 2012.

Wiesenthal, Simon. *The Sunflower: On the Possibilities and Limits of Forgiveness*. New York: Schocken, 2008.

Wilson, Marvin R. *Our Father Abraham: Jewish Roots of the Christian Faith*. Grand Rapids, Michigan: Eerdmans, 1989.

Yogananda, Paramhansa. *Autobiography of a Yogi*. New Dehli: Sterling, 2003.

Young, Brad H. *Jesus the Jewish Theologian*. Grand Rapids: Baker, 1993.

Made in the USA
Lexington, KY
10 March 2019